An Exposition of the *Epistle to the Romans*

IAN R. K. PAISLEY

AMBASSADOR
Belfast • Greenville

An Exposition of the *Epistle to the Romans*
Copyright © 1996 Ian R.K. Paisley
This edition 1996

ISBN 1 898787 71 9

Published by

AMBASSADOR PRODUCTIONS, LTD.
Providence House
16 Hillview Avenue,
Belfast, BT5 6JR

Emerald House
1 Chick Springs Road, Suite 102
Greenville, South Carolina, 29609

Foreword

THIS BOOK WAS written in the prison cell. It was a blessing when prepared and it was a blessing when it was first published. From all over the world have come letters of appreciation relating the uplift it has been to preachers and people alike.

When the jailer turned his key at night in my cell door I little thought that what I wrote in those long hours of solitary confinement would span the globe, nor did I think that I would serve in three Parliaments. But God does all things well. To God in Trinity and Trinity in Unity, the One Covenant God of Israel, I ascribe all the glory. May this library edition have upon it the dew of heaven.

Yours,
Set for the Defense
of the Gospel,
Ian R. K. Paisley
Eph 6 : 19 + 20

February 1996
Martyrs Memorial Church,
356-376 Ravenhill Road,
Belfast, BT6 8GL
Northern Ireland

THE
⋇ IAN R. K. PAISLEY LIBRARY ⋇

OTHER BOOKS IN THIS SPECIAL SERIES

♦ **Christian Foundations**

♦ **The Garments of Christ**

♦ **Sermons on Special Occasions**

♦ **Expository Sermons**

⋇ AVAILABLE FROM ⋇

AMBASSADOR PRODUCTIONS, LTD.

Providence House
16 Hillview Avenue,
Belfast, BT5 6JR
Telephone: 01232 658462

Emerald House
1 Chick Springs Road, Suite 102
Greenville, South Carolina, 29609
Telephone: 1 800 209 8570

Contents

1. **The gospel according** *to Paul* 7

2. **The Gentile and the Jew** *tried and condemned* 23

3. **The universal guilt, the universal guide,** *the universal gospel* . 33

4. **The test case of Abraham** *and its conclusion* 43

5. **The therefore of our justification** *and the wherefore
   of our identification* 51

6. **The science of our** *emancipation* 79

7. **The law** *of God* 103

8. **The chapter of** *the Spirit* 113

9. **The principle of** *Sovereign Grace* 137

10. **The preaching of** *Sovereign Grace* 145

11. **The purpose of** *Sovereign Grace* 157

12. **Our individual** *responsibility* 165

13. **Our social** *responsibility* 171

14. **Our fraternal** *responsibility* 175

15. **Our universal** *responsibility* 183

16. **The postscripts** *of the Epistle* 189

1 The gospel according *to Paul*

"Paul, a servant of Jesus Christ ... and the Lord Jesus Christ."

1. PAUL'S SERVITUDE

"A servant of Jesus Christ", v. 1. Servant in Greek "doulos" - slave.

(a) *The Purchase of the Slave*

Bought by his master's money. "Ye are not your own for ye are bought with a price", I Cor. 6:19, 20. The price is not silver or gold but the precious blood of the Lamb. Wondrous grace! So great a price for so worthless a person!

(b) *The Provision of the Slave*

He possesses nothing of his own. His garments are his master's. The slave's garments are usually of the poorest material. My Master has stripped off his Royal Robe of Righteousness and placed it on my shoulders. Blessed be His Name! The slave's food is his master's. How often do I desire other food than that of the Master's provision. How ungrateful I am! His food is the finest of the wheat. Everything he provides is of the best. What a Master! What a happy and contented slave I should be!

(c) *The Position of the Slave*

The slave is His Master's instrument. He has no will but His Master's. His is not to question but to obey.

Teach me, O Lord, to be a partaker of Thy Spirit, Thou Faithful Servant of Jehovah, who saidst, with the bloody sweat on Thy brow, "Not my will but thine be done".

2.   PAUL'S SEPARATION
"Separated unto the gospel of God", v.1.

(a) *The gospel of God's sovereignty separates the elect from the non-elect.*
(b) *The gospel of God's salvation separates the believer from the non-believer.*
(c) *The gospel of God's service separates the labourer from the loafer.*
(d) *The gospel of God's sanctification separates the saint from the sinner.*

Paul was a separatist. Gospel separation is separation by the gospel, according to the gospel, unto the gospel, for the gospel.

3.   PAUL'S SAVIOUR
Concerning His "Son, Jesus Christ our Lord …", vs. 2-6.

Paul's Saviour was:

(a) *A Promised Saviour*
"which He had promised afore by His prophets in the Holy Scriptures", v. 2.
(1) *The Revealer of the Promise*
"which He had", God Himself is the Revealer. God's secret is His Son. He is the Mystery of Godliness.
(2) *The Recipients of the Promise*
"afore by His prophets", the prophets were entrusted with the wonderful promise of the coming Christ.
(3) *The Record of the Promise*
"in the Holy Scriptures". The divine imprimatur is here placed on the Holy Scriptures. They and they alone are the divinely inspired record of God's dear son.

(b) *A Personal Saviour*
"Concerning his Son, Jesus Christ, our Lord", v.3.
There is a twofold relationship here.

(1) *A Divine relationship*

"His Son", His relationship to the Father.

(2) *A Human Relationship*

"Our Lord", His relationship to His people.

Note the link. What makes God's Son our Lord? His mediatorial work set forth in His titles Jesus and Christ. Jesus means *Saviour*, "Thou shalt call His name Jesus for He shall save His people from their sins" (Matt. 1:21).[1] Christ means "Anointed". "We have found the Messias (Hebrew) which is, being interpreted, the Christ (Greek anointed)" Jn 1:41; Cp. Can. 9:26; Ps. 2:2. He, as God's anointed, Prophet, Priest and King, has reconciled us unto God. So God's Son is *my* Lord. He is a personal Saviour.

(c) *A Powerful Saviour*

(1) *His Mysterious Incarnation*

"Was made of the seed of David according to the flesh", v. 3.

Here is proof of the eternal Sonship of Christ. He was God's Son but He was made according to the flesh of David's seed. Before His incarnation He was God's Son. He is the Eternal Son. Deity's Son is manifested in Davidic seed. Two natures joined in one person forever.

(2) *His Mighty Vindication*

"declared to be the Son of God with power, according to the Spirit of holiness, by the resurrection from the dead", v. 4.

The resurrection did not make Jesus Christ God's Son but it was a mighty vindication of what He already was. It was the vindication of His person and work, the topstone of glory on the great edifice of His mission.

The agency of the Resurrection was the Holy Ghost.[2]

[This section was written on the first day of imprisonment: Thursday, 21st July, 1966]

(3) *His Marvellous Salvation*

"By whom we have received grace and apostleship, for obedience to the faith among all nations, for His name: among whom are ye also the called of Jesus Christ," vs. 5 and 6.

(a) *The Reception of Salvation*

"we have received grace and apostleship", v. 5 (Jn. 1:12).

(b) *The Conception of Salvation*

"obedience to the faith among all nations", v. 5.

Man conceives of everybody being saved. God conceives the salvation of all the elect. The text does not say "obedience to the faith of all nations" but rather "obedience to the faith *among* all nations".

(c) *The Perception of Salvation*

"Among whom are ye also the called of Jesus Christ", v. 6.

Paul was able to perceive salvation in the believers in Rome. It is good to be saved and to know it but it is best to be saved and *show* it.

4.   PAUL'S SALUTATION

"To all that be in Rome, beloved of God, called to be saints: Grace to you and peace from God our Father, and the Lord Jesus Christ", v. 7.

(a) *The Saluted*

"To all that be in Rome, beloved of God, called to be saints."

(1) *Their Position Earthward*

"In Rome" our place of habitation is of God's predestination.

(2) *Their Position Godward*

"Beloved of God", John 17:3. "Beloved" - what a title! "Beloved of God" - what a testimony!

(3) *The Position Manward*

"Called Saints." Amongst darkened sinners we ought to shine as lights.

(b) *The Salutation*

"Grace to you and peace from God our Father, and the Lord Jesus Christ."

The two divine blessings from the two Divine Persons. Grace from God our Father, the source of all grace and peace from the Lord Jesus Christ, the Prince of Peace.

Both blessings are inseparable for both persons are inseparable. God is our Father. What solace we can draw from the Fatherhood of our God! Christ is our Lord. What solace we can draw from the Lordship of Christ! In the first we have affectionate protection characterised by mercy; in the second we have authoritative protection characterised by might.

[This section written on the second day of imprisonment: Friday, 22nd July, 1966]

SECOND SECTION: VERSES 8-17

In these verses we have Paul in four characteristic actions, Paul praising, Paul praying, Paul proposing and Paul preaching.

1.   PAUL PRAISING
"First, I thank my God through Jesus Christ for you all, that your faith is spoken of throughout the whole world." v. 8.

(a) *The Character of the Apostle's Praise*
    "I thank my God."

It was thankful praise. It rose from the deep well of gratitude to God within his heart. God was his God. He had entered into a never-to-be-forgotten covenant with Him. He knows God and is known of Him. His praise is intimate.

(b) *The Channel of the Apostle's Praise*
    "Through Jesus Christ"

Jesus Christ is the only channel to God for persons, prayers or praises. He is the only way to God the Father. No person can reach the Father's house but by Him. No prayer can reach the Father's throne but by Him and no praise can reach the Father's ear but by Him. The so-called praises of God by men with classical music and artistic performances are but the theatrical gimmicks of ecclesiastical showmen, a vain oblation of carnality with which the Almighty will have nothing to do.

(c) *The Content of the Apostle's Praise*
    "for you all".

All the believers in Rome filled up his praises. These called ones; these who were beloved of God, and these who were indeed the saints of the most High God. How we ought to praise God for His people. There is no people like the people of God.

(d) *The Compulsion of the Apostle's Praise*
    "that your faith is spoken of throughout the whole world."

He was compelled to praise God, for the faith of the church in Rome (not of Rome) had a universal testimony. Happy the church with a world-wide testimony for the faith once for all delivered unto the saints.

[This section written on the third day of imprisonment: Saturday, 23rd July, 1966]

2.   PAUL PRAYING
      "For God is my witness, whom I serve with my spirit in the gospel of His Son, that without ceasing I make mention of you always in my prayers; making request (if by any means now at length I might have a prosperous journey by the will of God) to come unto you."
      vs. 9 and 10.

(a) *The Witnessing of the Apostle's Prayers*
      "For God is my witness"
      Paul was no hypocrite. His prayers were not for public show like the Pharisees. His prayers were breathed in the secret place, known only to God were his long vigils at the throne of grace. Paul had learned to obey the command of our Lord Jesus Christ.
      "When thou prayest thou shalt not be as the hypocrites are: for they love to pray standing in the synagogues and in the corners of the streets, that they may be seen of men. Verily I say unto you, they have their reward.
      "But thou when thou prayest, enter into thy closet, and when thou has shut thy door, pray to the Father which is in secret; and thy Father which seeth in secret shall reward thee openly." (Matt. 6:5 and 6).
      God witnessed his prayers by giving his answer in a manner which cannot be gainsaid. Europe's gospel light and opportunity to this day are an answer to the Apostle's secret intercessions.

(b) *The Word of the Apostle's Prayers*
      "whom I serve with my spirit in the gospel of His Son", v. 9.
(1) *Prayer is Service*
      The highest form of service in the Old Testament was entrance within the veil. This was limited to the High Priest only and that once a year.
      The highest form of service in the New Testament is entrance within the veil in prayer. Every child of God has this privilege and that at all times. How we neglect this priceless privilege and blessed duty!
(2) *Prayer is Spiritual Service*
      "With my spirit."

Prayer is not a carnal performance done by the aids of the baubles of superstition (beads, candles, prayer wheels, etc.). Prayer is spiritual. It is man's redeemed spirit communicating with God who is spirit. It is deep calling unto deep; finite deep calling unto infinite deep. It is essentially something unseen and the unseen things are eternal.

Prayer is not the noisy sound which clamorous lips repeat. Prayer is the silence of the soul which clasps Jehovah's feet.

(3) *Prayer is Spiritual Service for the Son*

"in the gospel of His Son."

How easy it is to work in prayer when we have really learned the lesson of the Sunday School chorus, "We'll do it all for Jesus." It's for Him. We serve Him and as we love Him so, such service is blessedness indeed.

(c) *The Waiting of the Apostle's Prayers*

"That without ceasing I make mention of you in my prayers" v. 9.

He also serves who only stands and waits.

Waiting time is not wasted time. Note the words "without ceasing" and "always".

Prayer, like the altar fire in the Old Testament, must not cease but be burning brightly always. I must wait upon the Lord and patiently bear until He inclines His ear unto me.

(d) *The Want of the Apostle's Prayers*

"making request, if by any means now at length I might have a prosperous journey by the will of God to come unto you. For I long to see you, that I may impart unto you some spiritual gift, to the end ye may be established; that is, that I may be comforted together with you by the mutual faith both of you and me," vs. 10-12.

There are four wants in Paul's Prayers.

(i) *Paul wants to journey to them*

"If by any means now at length I might have a prosperous journey by the will of God to come unto you," v. 10.

"by any means."

Paul did not mind the means that would be used to get him to Rome. He eventually went there as a prisoner and a martyr. What did it matter - any means suited the apostle well.

"by the will of God."

Paul only wanted God's will. He had longed and waited but would not take a step outside the will of God.

"a prosperous journey."

Paul wanted a prosperous journey. He wanted spiritual prosperity to mark his whole journey to the Imperial City.

(ii) *Paul wants to meet them*

"For I long to see you", v. 11.

Paul wanted to meet those whom he often mentioned before God but who were (to use an expression of his own) "unknown by face" (Gal 1:22) to him. He longed to be intimately acquainted with all his brethren and sisters in the Lord. He wanted to know as many of the Lord's family personally as it was possible to know.

(iii) *Paul wants to edify them*

"That I may impart unto you some spiritual gift, to the end ye may be established," v. 11. Paul loved to be always giving. He learned by experience that the Lord loves a cheerful giver and that it is more blessed to give than to receive. He wanted the church to be established with all the gifts of the Holy Spirit. These are spiritual gifts, and not carnal. Only a spiritual church is an established church. A national name, human endowments and state recognition can establish a sect. Spiritual gifts alone establish a true church of Christ.

(iv) *Paul wants to comfort them*

"that I may be comforted together with you by the mutual faith both of you and me," v. 12.

The dark shadow of persecution was upon the church in Rome and also over the apostle's heart. He wanted to comfort them and to be comforted by God together with them that together they might stand the fiery trial that was to try both him and them.

A study of the Acts of the Apostles shows that all Paul's wants were met.

Paul journeyed in the will of God to Rome.

His journey though perilous was prosperous. God gave him all who sailed with him.

Paul met the Christians at Rome. He was able to establish the church there and together they were comforted in the fiery trial of martyrdom. God answers prayer.

3.   **PAUL PURPOSING**
       **"Now I would not have you ignorant, brethren, that oftentimes I purposed to come unto you (but was let hitherto) that I might have some fruit among you also, even as among other gentiles",
       v. 13.**

(a) *Paul's purpose revealed*

       "Now I would not have you ignorant, brethren". Paul wants the believers of Rome to know what is in his heart and on his mind. He reveals the great purpose of his soul. The great evangelist here uncovers the evangelistic purpose which possesses his whole being.

(b) *Paul's purpose resisted*

       "but was let hitherto" or hindered hitherto. No doubt Paul experienced Satanic resistance to his purpose "to preach the gospel to those who are at Rome also."

       Gospel purposes and gospel preachers will always be resisted as long as the Devil is out of the lake of fire.

(c) *Paul's purpose renewed*

       "that oftentimes I promised to come unto you."

       Paul was a determined man. He did not capitulate in the face of the enemy. What he purposed by God's help, in God's will and at God's time, he performed.

(d) *Paul's purpose restated*

       "that I might have some fruit among you also, even as among other Gentiles," v. 13.

       Paul's purpose was not selfish but rather spiritual. He yearned for souls. He saw the vast Imperial City as a great vineyard of souls and he purposed to gather fruit there for his Lord.

[This section written on the fourth day of imprisonment: Lord's day, 24th July, 1966]

4.   **PAUL PREACHING**
       "I am debtor both to the Greeks and to the Barbarians; both to the wise and to the unwise; so as much as in me is, I am ready to preach the gospel to you that are at Rome also.
       "For I am not ashamed of the gospel of Christ; for it is the power of God unto salvation to everyone that believeth; to the Jew first,

**and also to the Greek. For therein is the righteousness of God
revealed from faith to faith; as it is written, THE JUST SHALL LIVE
BY FAITH", vs. 14-16**

(a) *The Discharge of Preaching*

"I am debtor both to the Greeks and to the Barbarians, both to the wise
and to the unwise", v. 14.

Paul was a debtor. Preaching was the means by which the debt could be
discharged. It was a burden and he must unburden himself. To the Greeks, who
reckoned themselves wise and who sought after wisdom, he was in debt to preach
Christ the Wisdom of God. Equally to the Barbarians, who in ignorance knew not
what they sought, he was in debt to preach the same Christ, the wisdom of God.
To both the wise and the unwise he must preach the gospel.

(b) *The Desire of Preaching*

"I am ready to preach," v. 15.

"So, as much as in me is, I am ready to preach the gospel to you that are at
Rome also," v. 15.

Paul was a true preacher. He must preach, yea, woe was unto him if he
preached not the gospel.

He was ready to preach to everybody in every place, at every opportunity
and under every circumstance.

He could do nothing else but preach. When in prison he could not be
silenced but through his pen he preached the gospel round the world and to all
generations.

In the days of the great evangelical awakening a prominent Church of
England clergyman was reported to his bishop for preaching at times other than
those recognised by the laws of the established Church. Summoned before the
bishop the clergyman was asked, "How many times do you preach?" "Only two
times your lordship," was the quick reply. "When is that?" questioned the bishop,
"for I hear you are always preaching." "In season and out of season," retorted the
preacher.

Yes indeed, in season and out of season, that is when the true preacher is
at his business.

These silent sabbaths troubled the imprisoned Rutherford and they most
certainly trouble, at this very moment, the writer of these lines. Loyalty to Christ,
even if it entails silence, however, is far more important than the liberty of the

preacher. What we cannot preach we can nevertheless pen. For this we are indeed more than grateful to God and to the prison governor. In the vast majority of countries no such privilege would be ours.

(c) *The Defence of Preaching*

"I am not ashamed of the gospel of Christ," v. 16.

Paul was a defender both of the gospel and of the pulpit. He was unashamedly a preacher. He stood up for both his message and the means by which it was delivered. The message was divine and dynamic and the means of its delivery were also divine and dynamic.

Paul calls the message, "the power of God" in this first chapter of Romans and in the first chapter of First Corinthians he calls the means "the power of God".

"For the preaching of the cross is to them that perish foolishness; but unto us which are saved it is the power of God" (I Cor. 1:18).

He also maintains in this verse (verse 16) that the end of the gospel is the salvation of both Jew and Greek. In the first chapter of First Corinthians he maintains the very same of the preaching of the gospel. "It pleased God by the foolishness of preaching to save them that believe. For the Jews require a sign and the Greeks seek after wisdom: But we preach Christ crucified, unto the Jews a stumbling block, and unto the Greeks foolishness: But unto them which are called, both Jew and Greeks, Christ the power of God, and the wisdom of God" (I Cor 1:24). With Paul the gospel and its preaching could not be divorced. They were eternally united. The attempt to divorce them has wrought havoc with Twentieth Century Christianity. Today the pulpit is weak. Its authority is usurped. Consequently the church is paralysed. Ministers are good executives rather than good expositors. They do not give themselves to prayer and the ministry of the word like the early apostles. Preaching, the divinely appointed means, is discountenanced and the tragic results are evident. The church needs to return to preaching, old-fashioned, heaven-blessed, soul-stirring, sin-slaying preaching. The greatest need of the hour is a band of prophets with flaming message to set the land on fire.

The church's ministers today are mere clerical puppets on wire.

God's ministers are flames of fire.

The Reformation came through preaching. In Protestantism, apostolic and pure, the preacher displaced the priest. Today in Protestantism, apostate and corrupt, the priest has displaced the preacher. The Reformation is in reverse.

Such Protestantism falls an easy prey to the wolf of popery. This displacing of the preacher is manifested in modern church architecture. The pulpit no longer dominates for the modern cleric cannot preach. The central position is occupied by what is called the altar. The pulpit is pushed aside for the Word of God is rejected and a self-styled priest capable only of essay reading has taken the place of the preacher.

All true revivals are revivals of great preaching. When the trumpet of God really sounds then do sinners awaken from their slumbers of death. Oh for strength to blow the gospel trumpet!

(d) *The Dynamic of Preaching*

"for it is the power of God". v. 16.

Gospel preaching is charged with the dynamic of heaven. Dynamite, to be displayed in all its mighty potency, must have the fuse and the fire. When the fuse of true prayer is set alight with the fire of the Holy Ghost and thus the gospel dynamite is exploded, what tremendous results occur. Then do the strongholds of Satan topple. Then do the bulwarks of idolatry collapse. Then do the towering walls of sin suddenly fall. Then is the enemy dislodged. Then is all opposition blasted and the power of truth is proved to be more than conqueror. Oh for a day of real gospel preaching and gospel power! Lord let me witness such a day.

Human power stands impotent in the presence of the sins of our age. Divine power stands omnipotent over the sins of all ages. Oh for its mighty manifestation!

[This section written on the fifth day of imprisonment: Monday, 25th July, 1966]

(e) *The Design of Preaching*

"unto salvation to everyone that believeth: to the Jew first and also to the Greek," v. 16.

(i) *The Eternity of the* Design

"unto salvation".

The great design of preaching is the salvation of the soul. The preacher trafficks in immortal souls. He trades in the merchandise of eternity. His are not the matters of time, his are the matters of eternity. He labours not for the meat that perisheth. He labours for a harvest which will be reaped only in eternity.

Preaching is an eternal work. The wisdom of eternity is needed for its preparation. The solemnity of eternity is needed for its execution and the power of eternity is needed for its success.

(ii) *The Catholicity of the Design*

"to everyone that believeth".

The gospel has to be preached to all. Everyone who hears and believes shall be saved. The world is the gospel preacher's parish. He cannot be and will not be restricted. You could as soon stop the rising sun with a lollipop stick as stop the gospel preacher. No amount of opposition will stop him. He has a commission from heaven and must speak. His heart yearns to reach as many as he possibly can with the glad tidings of the gospel. Wesley had the true preacher's heart when he wrote:

"Oh, that the world might taste and see The riches of His grace. The arm of love that compass me would all mankind embrace."

The gospel is designed to be preached unto the whole wide world. It must be universally preached.

(iii) *The Priority of the Design*

"to the Jew first."

This is the divine priority. The preaching of the gospel to the Jew. It has been related of Samuel Chadwick that when he went to any town or city for a mission he enquired where the Jews were and made it his first business to proclaim Christ to them. In this he was not unmindful of the Lord's priority. How sadly the church of Jesus Christ has lost sight of the fact that the gospel is to the Jew first! Christian churches and the people argue over the future of the Jew but remain tragically unconcerned about the fate of the Jews around them. God help us to get our priorities right.

(iv) *The Impartiality of the Design*

"and also to the Greek."

The gospel design is impartial. There is no colour bar here. If the Jew is to hear the gospel first he has not to hear it alone. It is not an exclusive gospel but rather an inclusive one. Some are so interested "in the Jew first that they have forgotten the "and also to the Greek".

The design is not national but international irrespective of colour, class or creed. To all is this word of salvation sent.

(f) *The Doctrine of Preaching*

"For therein is the righteousness of God revealed from faith to faith: as it is written. "The Just Shall Live By Faith", v. 17.

The doctrine of preaching is here epitomised. In this verse we have the cream and essence, the pith and marrow of the message which the preacher heralds forth. The rest of the epistle goes on to expound it. The righteousness of God is contrasted with the sinfulness of man and then is revealed in its ordaining, justifying, sanctifying and glorifying work in the sinner's heart. The burden of the whole epistle is "THE JUST SHALL LIVE BY FAITH."

THIRD SECTION: VERSES 18-32

THE PIT OF MAN'S TOTAL DEPRAVITY UNCOVERED

The section starts with the terrors of God's wrath. The thunder-claps of divine indignation are heard and as we seek the reason for the revelation of this "wrath of God from heaven" verse 17, the pit of man's total depravity is uncovered and its loathsomeness lies exposed to our gaze.

(a) *The Descent of the Pit,* vs. 18-23.

Man's descent into the pit is carefully traced in these verses. Three major steps are here laid bare.

(i) *Ignorance*

"who hold the truth in unrighteousness. Because that which may be known of God is manifest in them; for God hath showed it unto them. For the invisible things of Him from the creation of the world are clearly seen, being understood by the things that are made, even His eternal power and God-head; so that they are without excuse; Because that, when they knew God, they glorified Him not as God," vs. 18-21.

This ignorance of man is his own workmanship. The light is shining but he deliberately puts it out or rather, unable to put it out, he puts out his own eyes so that he cannot see it, vs. 19 and 20. The truth challenges him and he takes it and turns it into his own condemnation and damnation by "holding it in unrighteousness", v. 18. We go down to the pit of depravity by that path of ignorance of our own devising.

(ii) *Ingratitude*

"neither were thankful," v. 21.

Base ignorance led to baser ingratitude. The goodness and longsuffering of God they abused by an unthankfulness begotten of hell itself. We who should have been loudest in our praises of God were loudest in our profanity of God.

(iii) *Idolatry*

"But became vain in their imaginations, and their foolish heart was darkened. Professing themselves to be wise, they became fools, and changed the glory of the incorruptible God into an image made like to corruptible man, and to birds, and four-footed beasts and creeping things," vs. 21 and 22.

Base ignorance leads to baser ingratitude and baser ingratitude leads to the basest idolatry. Sin is the root of idolatry. When Satan elevated himself and rejected the sovereignty of the most High he became the father of idolatry and idolaters. In idolatry holy things are usurped by the unholy, pure things are usurped by the impure and the incorruptible by the corrupt. Sin has made us all natural idolaters. We are as the result of the fall basically idol worshippers. We who should only bow before the God of heaven are found bent before the filthy shrines of the basest idolatries.

(b) *The Devilry of the Pit*

"Wherefore God also gave them up to uncleanness through the lusts of their own hearts, to dishonour their own bodies between themselves: who changed the truth of God into a lie, and worshipped and served the creature more than the Creator, who is blessed forever. Amen. For this cause God gave them up unto vile affections; for even their women did change the natural use into that which is against nature: and likewise also the men, leaving the natural use of the woman, burned in their lust one toward another; men with men working that which is unseemly, and receiving in themselves that recompense of their error which was meet," vs. 24-27.

Ignorance, ingratitude and idolatry produce the vilest immorality. Sin breaks forth in a hideous cancer, the stench of which reeks to the highest heaven. That which is designed and ordained of God for man's pleasure and comfort is perverted and abused until it becomes the vilest act and most debasing thing imaginable. The fire of the lust of the pit burns forth in a display of iniquity unmentionable. Womanhood is first debased and rejected and male with male sink down into the dark depths of the hell-hole of sodomy. Yes, and so corrupted are the very bishops and lawmakers of our land that such abominations are legalised.

Sin! Who can circumscribe thy devilry or exhaust thy devices?

(c) *The Depths of the Pit*

"And even as they did not like to retain God in their knowledge, God gave them over to a reprobate mind, to do those things which are not convenient;

being filled with all unrighteousness, fornication, wickedness, covetousness, maliciousness; full of envy, murder, debate, deceit, malignity; whisperers, backbiters, haters of God, despiteful, proud, boasters, inventors of evil things, disobedient to parents, without natural affection, implacable, unmerciful, who knowing the judgment of God that they which commit such things are worthy of death, not only do the same, but have pleasure in them that do them," vs. 28-32.

Paul here takes the plumbline and measures the depths of the pit of man's awful and total depravity. The divine spark theory is quenched forever in the darkness of this hell pit. Man is LOST! LOST! LOST!

(d) *The Damnation of the Pit*

"For the wrath of God is revealed from heaven against all ungodliness and unrighteousness of men," v. 18.

Damnation is the just reward of sinners. "To the lowest hell with such a vile brood" is the righteous sentence of inflexible justice. Wrath, wrath to the uttermost, is all we can expect. We are guilty and God's wrath consigns us to hell. We can only hang our heads and say "I deserve it". Lesser punishment would not be right.

[This section was written on the sixth day of imprisonment: Tuesday, 26th July, 1966]

Footnotes

1. Jesus, Hebrew Joshua or Jehoshua, compare Numbers 13:8, 16. "Oshea" meaning "salvation" in verse 8 is altered in verse 16 to "Jehoshua" Jehovah the Saviour.
2. Topic for a profitable Bible study, "The Agency of God the Holy Ghost in the Birth, Life, Ministry, Death and Resurrection of our Lord Jesus Christ". The Holy Ghost was active in Christ's birth. "That which is conceived in her (Mary) is of the Holy Ghost" (Matt. 1:20). Simeon's recognition of the Christ Child was by the Holy Ghost (Luke 2:25, 26). Both at our Lord's Baptism and Temptation the Holy Ghost's activity is noted (Matt. 3:16, 4:1). At the commencement of His Ministry His text was "The Spirit of the Lord is upon me" (Luke 4:18). His sacrifice was by the Holy ghost. "Who through the eternal Spirit offered himself without spot to God" (Heb. 9:14).

2 The Gentile and the Jew
tried and condemned

IN CHAPTER ONE, man is arrested and indicted by the law of God. The last verse of the first chapter records that terrible indictment. In chapter two man is on trial. This trial at the bar of God continues over into chapter three (v. 19) where the prisoners are all silenced and the just verdict of "guilty" is pronounced upon them.

The threshold of this chapter is the threshold of the courthouse of the law. The case is at hearing, the Crown v The World. Depositions are being taken for "the day when God shall judge the secrets of men, by Jesus Christ according to my gospel", v. 16.

The chapter divides itself into three parts.

(a) The Critic at the Bar, vs. 2-11.

(b) The Principle of the Judgment, vs. 12-16.

(c) The Jew at the Bar, vs 17-28.

(a) *The Critic at the Bar*

How man hates to be indicted. The indictment of the previous chapter galls his self-righteous soul, He is most indignant and has much to say for himself when he is first brought into court. He has constituted himself a judge in his own arrogance and pride.

Paul as the prosecuting counsel for the Crown soon silences Mr Talkative the Critic.

(i) *Paul argues that the judgment of God is according to truth.*

"But we are sure that the judgment of God is according to the truth against them which commit such things," v. 2.

The indictment is God's. He that searcheth the heart knoweth what it really contains. The secret places of the soul are naked and bare before His all-seeing, all-searching eye. How dare the impotent challenge the omnipotent. How dare the fool challenge the all-wise. How dare the sinful challenge the all-holy. The certainty that the judgment of God is according to truth is indisputable. The very nature of the case proves it. As God is the only true God and the God of truth, who cannot lie, how could His judgment be anything else than according to truth? Canst thou answer, prisoner at the bar? Nay, verily thou art silenced.

Again history confirms the fact that the judgment of God is according to truth. Prisoner at the bar, canst thou point out one judgment of God in history which was not according to truth? Nay, verily thou art silenced. The testimony of history without exception confirms that the judgment of God is according to truth.

Further, conscience concedes that the judgment of God is according to truth. Has conscience ever really indicted the God of truth of departing from the truth? Prisoner at the bar, in full light of that dread day, when God shall judge the secrets of thy heart by Jesus Christ according to my gospel, did your conscience ever witness that the judgment of God was not according to truth? Nay, verily thou art silenced. The universal testimony of conscience is that the judgment of God is according to truth.

[This section written on the seventh day of imprisonment: Wednesday, 27th July, 1966]

(ii) *Paul argues that by condemning others for the same offences the prisoner has condemned himself.*

"Therefore thou art inexcusable, O man, whosoever thou art that judgest: for wherein thou judgest another, thou condemnest thyself; for thou that judgest doest the same things," v. 1.

The prisoner has judged and condemned others for the very offences which he himself "practiseth" (better meaning for Greek word translated "doest"), and for which he now himself is judged. What defence, prisoner at the bar, canst thou offer? Over and over again thou hast roundly condemned these very offences in others. Thou art inexcusable.

(iii) *Paul argues that judgment is certain*

"And thinkest thou this, O man, that judgest them that do such things, and doest the same, that thou shalt escape the judgment of God", v. 3.

Thou who hast been so certain and so quick to judge others, thou thyself, God shall most certainly judge. God is not slack concerning his promise. Who hath hardened himself against God and prospered? There is no escape from God.

(iv) *Paul argues that the prisoner has aggravated his crime by rejecting the overtures of God's mercy.*

"or despisest thou the riches of His goodness and forbearance and long-suffering; not knowing that the goodness of God leadeth thee to repentance" v. 4.

The goodness of God the prisoner has despised. What God meant for his salvation he has abused for his greater damnation. God's goodness - the prisoner has wilfully interpreted as God's weakness and made it an excuse for greater sinnings.

The forbearance of God - the prisoner has despised God's forbearance and has wilfully misinterpreted it as God's unconcern for sin. Because God forbears the prisoner perseveres in the course of evil.

The long-suffering of God the prisoner has despised. Because God has not damned him instantly he wilfully interprets that God will not damn him at all. What was meant for his repentance he uses for his reprobation. Repentance is far from his mind. He refuses to repent and like the profane Esau for a morsel of meat sells his birthright.

(v) *Paul argues that the prisoner is heaping up wrath against the day of wrath,* v. 5.

"But after thy hardness and impenitent heart treasurest up unto thyself wrath against the day of wrath and revelation of the righteous judgment of God."

The prisoner's hard and impenitent heart is such proof of his guilt that wrath is his just portion. In fact the prisoner is so corrupted that he refuses "the riches" of God (v. 4) and makes his treasure the "wrath" of God. Note the sharp contrast. The prisoner's labour is to treasure up wrath against the day of wrath. What an occupation! What awful retribution!

(vi) *Paul argues the doctrine of recompense.*

"Who will render to every man according to his deeds. To them who by patient continuance in well-doing seek for glory and honour and immorality, eternal life: But unto them that are contentious, and do not obey the truth, but obey unrighteousness, indignation and wrath, tribulation and anguish," vs. 6-9.

The day of recompense is sure. Those who are saved shall be eternally separated from those who are lost. For the saved shall have glory and honour and incorruptibility and those who are lost shall have indignation, wrath, tribulation and anguish. The prisoner has not "by patient continuance in well-doing sought for glory etc." v. 7. Therefore the portion of the lost shall be his. The two ways and the two destinies are here made unmistakably clear. The prisoner having walked the way to hell must certainly end there. The way to hell does not terminate in heaven.

(vii) *Paul argues that there is no respect of persons with God.*

"Tribulation and anguish upon every soul of man that doeth evil, of the Jew first and also of the Gentile; but glory, honour, and peace, to every man that worketh good, to the Jew first, and also to the Gentile. For there is no respect of persons with God," vs. 9-11.

Not who he is but what he is, constitutes the sole consideration at the judgment. Men can "square themselves" out from under man's laws but from under God's laws, never. There is no respect of persons with God.

The critic represents the whole Gentile world. That world at its cleverest is justly condemned. The prisoner at the bar overwhelmed in his own confusion cannot answer the case for the Crown. Every Gentile is rightly indicted and righteously condemned. In God's holy presence I can only bow and say, "I am totally depraved and am fit only for hell. I am guilty! Guilty! Guilty!"

***[This section written on the eighth day of imprisonment:
Thursday, 28th July, 1966]***

(b) *The Principle of the Judgment*, vs. 12-16.

"For as many as have sinned without law shall also perish without law: and as many as have sinned in the law shall be judged by the law (for not the hearers of the law are just before God but the doers of the law shall be justified). For when the Gentiles, which have not the law, do by nature the things contained in the law, these, having not the law, are a law unto themselves: Which show the work of the law written in their hearts, their conscience also bearing witness, and their thoughts the meanwhile accusing or else excusing one another.

"In the day when God shall judge the secrets of men by Jesus Christ according to my gospel", vs. 12-16.

(i) *The Principle of the Judgment is Fair.*

"For as many as have sinned without law shall also perish without law: and as many as have sinned in the law shall be judged by the law," v. 12.

The judge of all the earth shall do right. Those without the revelation of the law, the moral law as summed up in the ten commandments, shall be judged according to the moral law as written in their hearts. As sinners they shall perish but they shall be as Sodom and Gomorrah in judgment compared with those who heard the Saviour and rejected Him. Of such the Saviour, Himself, said, "Verily, I say unto you, it shall be more tolerable for Sodom and Gomorrah in the day of judgment, than for that city" (Mark 6:11).

(ii) *The Principle of the Judgment is Faithful*

("For not the hearers of the law are just before God, but the doers of the law shall be justified. For when the Gentiles, which have not the law, do by nature the things contained in the law, these, having not the law, are a law unto themselves. Which shew the work of the law written in their hearts, their conscience also bearing witness and their thoughts the mean while accusing or else excusing one another,") vs. 13-15.

In this parenthesis the principle of the judgment is further expounded. The principle of the judgment is faithful, that is true to fact. It is not the hearers of the law who stand justified but rather the doers. Those Gentiles who never received the revelation of the law as contained in the Old Testament scriptures will not be judged by something they have not received.

In their hearts is, however, engraven the divine law and although they have not the letter of the law yet they have its matter and by that, written within their hearts, they shall be judged. Even already their conscience testifies to the faithful principle of the judgment by either accusing or else excusing them.

(iii) *The Principle of the Judgment is Final*

"In the day when God shall judge the secrets of men by Jesus Christ according to my gospel" v. 16.

Verses 13-15 form a parenthesis as we have already noted. We must read verse 12 to get the direct context of verse 16.

We read thus: "For as many as have sinned without law shall also perish without law: and as many as have sinned in the law shall be judged by the law; in the day when God shall judge the secrets of men by Jesus Christ according to my gospel," vs. 12, 16.

The principle of the judgment is final. There is no redress from its application on the dread day of judgment.

It shall be applied "by Jesus Christ".

It shall be applied in the manner stated here by Paul the Apostle, "according to my gospel". It shall be applied for and on behalf of God, "God shall judge".

It shall be applied to "the secrets of men".
"In the day" - What an Expectation!
"God shall judge" - What an Experience!
"the secrets of men" - What an Exposure!
"by Jesus Christ" - What an Executor!
"according to my gospel" - What an Examination!

[This section was written on the ninth day of imprisonment: Friday, 29th July, 1966]

(c) *The Jew at the Bar,* vs. 17-18.

Having arrested, indicted and proved conclusively the guilt of the Gentile, Paul now indicts and proves conclusively the guilt of the Jew. The Jew stands proudly at the bar. He trusts in his lineage and in his understanding of the law. He comes into court a religious braggart, confident in his own righteousness and indignant that any charge should dare to be levelled against him.

Paul as prosecuting counsel,

(i) Examines the Jew's Privileges, vs. 17-20.

(ii) Exposes the Jew's Practices, vs. 21-24.

(iii) Expounds the Jew's Position, vs. 25-29.

(i) *His Privileges Examined,* vs. 17-20

The prisoner at the bar is a unique person. He has privileges far beyond the cleverest Gentile. If ever a man should not be found in court this man should not be found there. He has not sinned against a little natural light but against the greatest spiritual light.

Paul argues the privilege of the Jews *Lineage.*

"Behold thou art called a Jew", v. 17.

He came of a chosen race. He was of God's own peculiar people according to the flesh. He could trace his lineage back to Abraham the friend of God, the father of the faithful and the founder of the nation.

Paul as Saul once stood in his position and made a similar boast. After the grace of God had transformed him he could write - "Though I might also have confidence in the flesh. If any other man thinketh that he hath whereof he might trust in the flesh, I more:

Circumcised the eighth day, of the stock of Israel, of the tribe of Benjamin, an Hebrew of the Hebrews; as touching the law a Pharisee; concerning zeal, persecuting the church; touching the righteousness which is in the law, blameless:" - Phil. 3:4-6.

All the background of the Jew ought to have led him to God but he had wilfully, deliberately and consistently gone away from God. His lineage had become for him a cloak by which he sought to conceal his iniquity and perversity. He had sinned against the light of his own lineage.

Paul argues the privilege of the Jew's *Knowledge*.

"And restest in the law, and makest thy boast of God, and knowest His will, and approvest the things that are more excellent, being instructed out of the law", vs. 17, 18.

The prisoner cannot plead ignorance of the law of God.

He maintains that its principles are his foundation, "restest in the law"; its Giver is his boast, "makest thy boast of God"; its precepts are his enlightenment, "Knowest his will", and its excellency is his choice, "approvest the things that are more excellent", all because he has knowledge of its truth, "being instructed out of the law".

The prisoner's knowledge of the law ought to have led him to virtue but instead he made it a cloak for his vice.

Paul argues the privilege of the Jew's *Advantage*.

"And art confident that thou thyself art a guide of the blind, a light of them which are in darkness, an instructor of the foolish, a teacher of babes, which hast the form of knowledge and of the truth in the law:" vs. 19, 20.

The prisoner at the bar has not the knowledge of the law of God as a mere scholar; he, of his own confession, is a teacher of that law. He is confident that his rightful place is not that of receiving instruction but rather of giving it. He boldly professes to have such a grasp of "the form and knowledge of the truth in the law" that he is

"a guide of the blind" "a light of them which are indarkness" "an instructor of the foolish" and "a teacher of babes."

He has the great advantage of being a teacher of the law.

How guilty he is!

He has abused this advantage to his own destruction.

His privileges of lineage, knowledge and advantage which are steps to heaven he makes into steps to hell.

(ii) *His Practices Exposed*, vs. 21-24.

Paul exposes the corrupt practices of the prisoner by five devastating questions. These uncover

The hypocrisy of the Jew

"Thou therefore which teachest another, teachest thou not thyself?" v. 21.

The prisoner taught others but did not himself heed his own instructions. He was wilfully blind himself though he taught the blind. He stayed in darkness himself though he enlightened those who were in darkness. He was deliberately a fool himself though he instructed the foolish. He was like the father who thrashed his son for cursing, while himself blaspheming. The prisoner at the bar has no answer to this question. He is silent. He is indeed guilty of hypocrisy.

The iniquity of the Jew

"Thou that preachest a man should not steal, dost thou steal?"

"Thou that sayest a man should not commit adultery, dost thou commit adultery?" "Thou that abhorrest idols, dost thou commit sacrilege?" vs. 21. 22. Man can sin against his fellows, against himself and against his God. The Jew has sinned in all three directions. When the question is put, "Dost thou steal? he is silent. Guilt is written upon his countenance. Stealing is a sin against his fellows. He has sinned in this direction. When the question is put, "Dost thou commit adultery?" he is silent. Confusion overwhelms him. Adultery is a sin against his body, against himself.

"Every sin that a man doeth is without the body: but he that committeth fornication sinneth against his own body", I Cor. 6:18. Again when the question is put, "Dost thou commit sacrilege?" the accused is still silent. Condemnation is more than evident. Sacrilege is a sin against God. The accused is still silent. Condemnation is more than evident. Sacrilege is a sin against God. The accused has sinned in this direction.[1] Against his fellows, against himself and against his God. Such is the totality of the Jew's iniquity.

The braggart is now silent. His boasting is gone. He stands condemned at the bar of that law in which he claimed he rested.

The blasphemy of the Jew

"Thou that makest thy boast of the law, through breaking the law dishonourest thou God?"

"for the name of God is blasphemed among the Gentiles through you, as it is written:" vs. 23, 24.

The Jew is guilty of blasphemy. By boasting of the law and at the same time breaking it, he dishonoured the God of heaven and caused the enemies of God to blaspheme God's holy name.

Paul refers to Holy Scripture "as it is written", to confirm this. The reference is undoubtedly to the prophecy of Ezekiel 36:20-23.

"And when they entered unto the heathen, whither they went, they profaned My holy name, and when they said to them, These are the people of the

Lord, and are gone forth out of His land. But I had pity for Mine holy name, which the house of Israel had profaned among the heathen, whither they went."

"Therefore say unto the house of Israel. Thus saith the Lord God; I do not this for your sakes, O house of Israel, but for Mine holy name's sake, which ye have profaned among the heathen, whither ye went.

"And I will sanctify My great name, which was profaned among the heathen, which ye have profaned in the midst of them; and the heathen shall know that I am the Lord, saith the Lord God, when I shall be sanctified in you before their eyes."

Not only had Paul the scattered nation in mind but also David in his sin. In the next chapter at verse three he quotes David's prayer of repentance, Psalm 51: 4. Remember what was said of David's sin, "By this deed thou hast given great occasion to the enemies of the Lord to blaspheme" (II Sam. 12:14).

Even unto this day David's sin causes the enemies of God to blaspheme.

This is the depth of the sin of the Jew. He is the producer of blasphemy against the God he professes to know and serve.

(iii) *His Position Explained*

"For circumcision verily profiteth, if thou keep the law; but if thou be a breaker of the law, thy circumcision is made uncircumcision."

"Therefore if the uncircumcision keep the righteousness of the law, shall not his uncircumcision be counted for circumcision? And shall not uncircumcision which is by nature, if it fulfil the law, judge thee, who by the letter and circumcision dost transgress the law."

"For he is not a Jew, which is one outwardly; neither is that circumcision, which is outward in the flesh."

"But he is a Jew, which is one inwardly; and circumcision is that of the heart, in the spirit and not in the letter; whose praise is not of men but of God," vs. 25-29. After the condemnation of the Gentile we have a section dealing with the Gentile's position at the judgment, see verses 12-16.

Now at the conclusion of the condemnation of the Jew we have this section which explains the Jew's position at the judgment. These verses then are complementary to verses 12-16. The law is seen here in all its spirituality. Circumcision, a sign, is put in its proper place. The inward grace, signified by the outward sign, is the one thing needful. To wear the sign and not partake of the grace signified is useless. The real Jew is inward and not outward. The true circumcision is not of the flesh but of the spirit, not discernable by men but by God.

The guilty Jew as a breaker of the law has made his circumcision uncircumcision; and the uncircumcised must be cut off from the people.

"And the uncircumcised man child whose flesh of his foreskin is not circumcised, that soul shall be cut off from his people; he hath broken my covenant (Gen. 17:14).

This is the Jew's true position.

In the next chapter Paul concludes the case against the Jew and the verdict is then pronounced upon both Jew and Gentile.

[This section was completed on the twelfth day of imprisonment: Monday, 1st August, 1966, the 20th Anniversary of my ordination to the ministry of the gospel in Ravenhill]

Footnotes

1. It must, of course, be remembered that all sin is, in the final analysis, against God. The nature of sin is rebellion against the most High God no matter what direction it takes. Thus David who sinned against his fellows and his body must cry "Against Thee, Thee only, have I sinned" (Ps. 51:4).

3 The universal guilt,
the universal guide,
the universal gospel

IN THE LAST section of the previous chapter we noted, (1) The Jew's privileges Examined, (2) The Jew's Practices Exposed and (3) The Jew's Position Explained. IN verse 1-8 of this chapter the section on the Jew is concluded with His Penalty Expounded. The remainder of the chapter verses 9-31 deal with (1) verse 20, and (3) The Universal Gospel, verses 21-31.

(4) *The Jew's Penalty Expounded*

"What advantage then hath the Jew? or what profit is there of circumcision?"

"Much every way: chiefly, because that unto them were committed the oracles of God. For what if some did not believe? Shall their unbelief make the faith of God without effect? God forbid: yea, let God be true, but every man a liar; as it is written, That thou mightest be justified in thy sayings, and mightest overcome when thou art judged. But if our unrighteousness commend the righteousness of God, what shall we say? Is God unrighteous who taketh vengeance? (I speak as a man.) God forbid: for then how shall God judge the world?

"For if the truth of God hath more abounded through my lie unto his glory; why yet am I also judged as a sinner? And not rather, (as we be slanderously reported, and as some affirm that we say) Let us do evil, that good may come?

whose damnation is just" - verses 1-8. Three expressions give us the key to this portion, "The faith; i.e. the faithfulness of God", verse 3, "the righteousness of God", verse 5, and "the truth of God", verse 7.

The Penalty of the Jew vindicates:

The Faithfulness of God

The oracles of God were committed to the Jewish race. In these oracles were revealed promises of grace and warnings of judgment. The Jews had this advantage over the Gentiles. God's word was with them. Their unbelief or unfaithfulness could not undermine the faithfulness of God. God is faithful who promised. He also will do it. The promises of wrath upon His disobedient people must fall. His faithfulness will be vindicated either in grace or, if grace is rejected, then in judgment.

The Righteousness of God

Justice demands punishment. God's righteousness can only be vindicated by the punishment of sin. The soul that sinneth must surely die. The sinful Jew must be punished, for God's character must be manifested in its eternal righteousness. It is only right that such a prisoner should be punished.

"Is God unrighteous who taketh vengeance?" asks the apostle in verse 5. The answer is "God forbid; for then how shall God judge the world?"

The Truth or Holiness of God

"Let God be true, but every man a liar" v. 4. God's holiness demands the judgment of sin. God's character must be manifested not only in eternal faithfulness, eternal righteousness, but also in eternal holiness. The apostle goes back to the experience of David and quotes Psalm 51.

The whole 4th verse reads:

"Against Thee, Thee only, have I sinned and done this evil in thy sight; that Thou mightest be justified when thou speakest, and be clear when thou judgest."

Sin is essentially an attack on the holiness of God and God's holiness can only be vindicated by its punishment.

The punishment of the Jew then, is not merely an act of eternal retribution but rather an act of eternal righteousness, faithfulness and truth.

[This section completed on the fifteenth day of imprisonment: Thursday 4th August, 1966]

1.   THE UNIVERSAL GUILT, vs. 9-19

In these verses we have the momentous conclusion of the great law suit.

Both Jew and Gentile are in the dock. Paul as Crown counsel is finishing the case. The Word of God enthroned on the seat of justice will sum up and the verdict will be announced.

(a) *The Case Proved*

"What then? are we better than they? No, in no wise; for we have before proved both Jews and Gentiles, that they are all under sin" v. 9.

The case against both Jew and Gentile has been fully proved. The arguments of Paul are irrefutable. Every conceivable point has been taken and clearly and fully elucidated. The defendants' position has been totally shattered and their guilt has been demonstrated up to the hilt. Paul the able advocate takes his seat, the case for the Crown is closed.

(b) *The Judge Sums Up*

"As it is written:

1. There is none righteous, no not one:
2. There is none that understandeth.
3. There is none that seeketh after God.
4. They are all gone out of the way.
5. They are altogether become unprofitable.
6. There is none that doeth good, no, not one.
7. Their throat is an open sepulchre.
8. With their tongues they have used deceit.
9. The poison of asps is under their lips.
10. Whose mouth is full of cursing and bitterness.
11. Their feet are swift to shed blood.
12. Destruction and misery are in their ways.
13. And the way of have they peace know known.
14. There is no fear of God before their eyes." vs. 10-18.

The Word of God enthroned on the seat of justice sums up. Let it ever be remembered that the Word of God Incarnate by the Word of God inspired will be the final judge of all men and angels.

In Revelation chapter nineteen we see the heaven opened and one come forth to *judge* and His name is "The Word of God" (Rev. 19:11-13).

In Revelation chapter twenty this one who has come forth judges those brought before him out of those things which were written in the opened books. Rev. 20:12. What books? Why, none other than the books of the Old and New Testaments. The Word of God is the sole judge.

The Word of God sums up the case in fourteen stern conclusions. These are worthy of careful consideration. These conclusions are in seven pairs, (It need hardly be pointed out that seven is the perfect number. The judgment of the Word of God is perfect judgment) and it will be seen by a little careful study that the pairs do not go together. In fact the first and the last, the fourteenth, form a pair, the second and the thirteenth, the third and the twelfth and so on. Their relationship is easily seen when we place them together.

1st pair

v. 10 "There is none righteous, no, not one!"

v. 18 "There is no fear of God before their eyes."

The fear of God is the beginning of wisdom. Without this fear how can man have any righteousness? But these have no fear of God therefore none is righteous, no, not one.

2nd pair

v. 11 "There is none that understandeth."

v. 17 "And the way of peace have they not known."

Having not known the way of peace it can be rightly said they have no understanding. Ignorance of the way of peace makes a man a fool indeed.

3rd pair

v. 11 "There is none that seeketh after God."

v. 16 "Destruction and misery are in their ways."

These characteristics of their path, destruction and misery, prove that they seek not after God.

4th pair

v. 12 "They are all gone out of the way."

v. 15 "Their feet are swift to shed blood."

Their path being one of swift blood-shedding proves that they are out of the way i.e. the way of God.

5th pair

v. 12 "They are together become unprofitable."

v. 14 "Whose mouth is full of cursing and bitterness."

How could they be anything else but unprofitable when their mouth knows no other fullness but that of cursing and bitterness?

6th pair

v. 12 "There is none that doeth good, no not one."

v. 13 "The poison of asps is under their lips."

The poisoned lip is but the sign-post of the poisoned life. Like lips, like life, lips no good, life no good.

7th pair

v. 13 "Their throat is an open sepulchre."

v. 13 "With their tongues have they used deceit."

Their deceitful tongues reveal the death cell of their corrupted throats.

It should be noted that the second line of each pair gives the proof of the first line as we have sought to point out in our brief comments thereon. For example, as there is no fear of God before their eyes, therefore there is none righteous no, not one; as the way of peace they have not known, therefore there is none that understandeth etc., etc.

This is the terrible summing up. The first pair is a condemnation of the corrupt *heart* of both Jew and Gentile. The second pair is a condemnation of their corrupt *understanding*. The third pair is a condemnation of their corrupted *motives*. The fourth is a condemnation of their corrupted *walk*. The fifth is a condemnation of their corrupted *practices* and the seventh is a condemnation of their corrupted *character*.

These seven pairs form a complete synopsis of the indictments of the apostle in chapters one and two. Paul traces from verse 21 of chapter one how they put away the fear of God from before their eyes and went down and down and down until their mouth became an open sepulchre and with their tongues they used deceit, 2:22. Not only have their sins been found out but their sins have found them out.

(c) *The Verdict Announced*

"Now we know that what things soever the law saith, it saith to them who are under the law: that every mouth may be stopped and all the world may become guilty before God" v. 19. The whole world guilty, that is the verdict. There is no exception. All have sinned and all are guilty. Paul has already shown that Jew and Gentile are under the law, the Jew under the law written by the finger of God on the tables of stone and the Gentile under the same law written by the same finger on the tables of his heart.

Have the prisoners anything to say before sentence is passed upon them? No, their mouths are stopped, they stand speechless before their Maker.

[This section completed on the 18th day of imprisonment: Lord's Day, 7th August, 1966]

2   THE UNIVERSAL GUIDE
"Therefore by the deeds of the law there shall no flesh be justified in His sight; for by the law is the knowledge of sin" v. 20.

Here we have the universal guide to sinners, both Jews and Gentiles. Sinful man has his own conceited ideas but the plain statements of this verse form a sure guide-post, warning the seeker how he can find peace with his Maker.

(a) *Deliverance from the Law - Imperative*
"Justified in His sight."
The law is spiritual but we are carnal, sold under sin.
Because of the weakness of the flesh the law is a terror, a curse to our souls.
It brings us into bondage and imprisonment. It was first written upon tables of stone signifying that its precepts are stern and cold.
From its curse we must be delivered; from its imprisonment we must be freed; from it slavery we must be emancipated, and from its sentence we must be justified. If we are to escape the death which never dies it is imperative that we be delivered from the law and its curse.

(b) *Deeds of the Law - Impotent*
"Therefore by the deeds of the law there shall no flesh be justified."
The deeds of the law are impotent to justify. There is no exception to this rule, it governs all flesh. The deeds i.e. the works of the law, cannot save. This rules out all the efforts of man. So darkened is the sinful soul of man that he refuses to heed the universal guidance of our text. The works of the law form the very heart of man's religion. Proud man wants to work for his salvation. In Christian lands he makes the church and its ceremonies into the way of salvation and proudly strives to justify himself by ceremonial and church works. Our text strikes the death knell of man's religion. By the deeds of the law, moral, religious or charitable, no flesh can be justified in God's sight. Salvation is not of works lest any man should boast. Works! Works! You could as soon fly to heaven astride a straw as get there by your own good works. The Deeds of the Law are indeed *Impotent*.

(c) *Design of the Law - Important*

"For by the law is the knowledge of sin. The word for knowledge here signifies full knowledge. Further on in the epistle Paul expounds the character and purpose of the law and its present standing in the believer's life. Enough now to emphasise that the Design of the Law is *Important* and its importance must not be minimised.

3   THE UNIVERSAL GOSPEL, vs. 21-31.

In these eleven verses we have a summary of the Gospel which Paul fully expounds in the following chapters. These verses are indeed a table of contents of the following chapters. Verse 21 speaks of "Righteousness of God without the law is manifested, being witnessed by the law and prophets". The fourth chapter fully expounds this theme and refers to Abraham, whose life is recorded in the first book of the law, Genesis, and David whose life is recorded in the books of the Prophets according to the Hebrew division of the Old Testament.[1]

Verse 24 speaks of "being justified freely by His grace through the redemption that is in Christ Jesus". These truths of justification, grace and redemption are expounded in chapters five and six.

In chapters seven and eight the themes of verses 26-28 are fully elucidated.

The question of verse 29, "Is He the God of the Jews only? Is He not also of the Gentiles?" is fully answered in chapters nine, ten and eleven. The "Yea, we establish the law", of verse 31 is proved in the final chapters of the epistle, chapters twelve to sixteen.

The remainder of the epistle then is an exposition of the Universal Gospel.

Chapter one to chapter three verse twenty expounds man's ruin.

Chapter three verse twenty-one to chapter sixteen expounds God's remedy i.e. the universal good news of redemption in Christ Jesus.

The great theme of the universal gospel is "Righteousness without the law".

In verse 21-23 we have this righteousness revealed by the Word; in verse 24-26 we have the righteousness declared by the Son and in verse 27-31 we have this righteousness received by faith.

(a) *"Righteousness without the Law" - Revealed by the Word.*

"But now the righteousness of God without the law is manifested, being witnessed by the law and the prophets."

"Even the righteousness of God which is by faith of Jesus Christ unto all and upon all them that believe: for there is no difference. For all have sinned and come short of the glory of God" - vs. 21-23.

The Word of God most certainly reveals

(1) *The necessity of this righteousness.*

Verse 23 is quite sufficient to prove that. All have sinned and come short of the glory of God. Lost in sin, unable by the deeds of the law to save himself, righteousness without the law is a due necessity for man.

The word of God most certainly reveals

(2) *The notion² of this righteousness.*

Verse 21 speaks of it being "witnessed by the law and the prophets". The fourth chapter fully expands this as we have already noted. The Word of God most certainly reveals

(3) *The nature of this righteousness.*

Verse 22 tells us that it is "the righteousness of God which is by faith of Jesus Christ unto all and upon all them that believe".

(1) *Its source* is God, it is "the righteousness of God".

(2) *Its substance* is Jesus Christ, it is "of Jesus Christ".

(3) *Its science* is faith, it is "by faith".

(4) *Its scope* is believers, it is "upon all them that believe".

[This section completed on the nineteenth day of imprisonment: Monday, 8th August, 1966]

(b) *"Righteousness Without the Law" - Declared by the Son.*

"Being justified freely by His grace through the redemption that is in Christ Jesus."

"Whom God hath set forth to be a propitiation through faith in His blood, to declare His righteousness for the remission of sins that are past, through the forbearance of God; To declare, I say, at this time His righteousness: that He might be just, and the justifier of him which believeth in Jesus", vs. 24-26.

The righteousness without the law is declared by

(1) *redemption.*

V. 24 "Being justified freely by His grace through the redemption that is in Christ Jesus."

God's Son in redemption declared a "righteousness without the law" which by grace through faith freely justifies the believer.

(2) *remission*

V. 25 "To declare His righteousness for the remission of sins."

The remission of sins by God's Son through the propitiation of His precious blood declares "a righteousness without the law".

(3) *reconciliation*

V. 26 "That He might be just, and the justifier of him which believeth in Jesus."

The reconciliation of two seemingly contradictory propositions, that God can be just and at the same time justify the sinner by Jesus Christ on the cross declares his "righteousness without the law" not merely a possibility but an actuality. At Calvary, mercy and truth embraced and righteousness and peace kissed each other, (Ps. 85:10).

(c) *"Righteousness without the Law" - Received by Faith*

"Where is boasting then? It is excluded. By what law? of works? Nay; but by the law of faith."

"Therefore we conclude that a man is justified by faith without the deeds of the law."

"Is He the God of the Jews only? Is He not also of the Gentiles? Yes, of the Gentiles also: 'Seeing it is one God which shall justify the circumcision by faith and the uncircumcision through faith'."

"Do we then make void the law through faith? God forbid: yea, we establish the law!" - vs. 27-31.

The "righteousness without the law" must be received by faith

(1) *for the glory must be God's alone*

V. 27 "Where is boasting then? It is excluded."

It is by faith, not of works lest any man should boast. Only by the law of faith can the glory be given to God alone.

The "righteousness without the law" must be received by faith

(2) *for God is God of both Jew and Gentile.*

V. 30 "Seeing it is one God."

If the Gentiles have not the written law, and the Jews have it but cannot be justified through it, how better can God be shown to be the one God of both than by justifying them in the same manner. By what law? The law of faith.

The "righteousness without the law" is received by faith.

(3) *for the law must be established.*

V. 31 "Yea, we establish the law."

Breaking the law dishonours it. The law is established in its fulfilment. How better could it be fulfilled than by Jesus Christ our Lord?

Through faith, His righteousness i.e. His fulfilment of the law, is mine and so the law is established.

[This section completed on the twentieth day of imprisonment: Tuesday, 9th August, 1966)

Footnotes

1. Divisions of the Hebrew Bible. The Jews divided their sacred books into three parts:
1. "The Law" (Tôrâh), comprising the five books of Moses.
2. "The Prophets" (Nebiim), comprising the Books of Joshua, Judges, I and II Samuel, I and II Kings, Isaiah, Jeremiah, Ezekiel, and the twelve Minor Prophets.
3   "The Writings" (Kethubim). Under this title were placed:
(1) Psalms, Proverbs, Job.
(2) Song of Solomon, Ruth, Lamentations, Ecclesiastes, Esther.
(3) Daniel, Ezra, Nehemiah, I and II Chronicles.
2. I use the word "notion" as meaning "conception".

4 The test case of Abraham
and its conclusion

WE HAVE DISCOVERED that verses 21-31 of the previous chapter are in fact a table of contents of the chapters which follow. Verse 21 speaks of "the righteousness of God without the law, being witnessed by the law and the prophets" and in this chapter we have the theme fully expanded and explained.

This chapter is the chapter of "the test case of Abraham and its conclusion".

The test case of Abraham, vs. 1-22.

The conclusion, vs. 22.25.

1   THE TEST CASE OF ABRAHAM, vs 1-22

The case has four sections.

(a) Abraham's discovery, vs . 1-8.

(b) Abraham's designation, vs. 9-12.

(c) Abraham's destiny, vs. 13-17.

(d) Abraham's determination, vs. 18-21.

(a) *Abraham's discovery came by revelation*

"What shall we say then that Abraham our father, as pertaining to the flesh, hath found? For if Abraham were justified by works, he hath wereof to glory; but not before God. For what saith the scripture? Abraham believed God, and it was counted unto him for righteousness."

"Now to him that worketh is the reward not reckoned of grace, but of debt."

"But to him that worketh not, but believeth on him that justifieth the ungodly, his faith is counted for righteousness" (Rom. 4:1-5).

Justification by faith alone is a revealed doctrine. Abraham found it out in communion with God. He learned that he had nothing to glory of, that his justification was not the reward of his working reckoned as the payment of debt (verse 4) but rather the free gift of grace. He believed God and it was reckoned, i.e. placed to his account, for righteousness. What did he believe? He believed in the promise of the son which God was going to give him, a type of God's own Son given for the world.

In that son was the great incident of Mt. Moriah where the faith of Abraham had its fullest expression. Of the faith thus expressed, our Lord Jesus Christ could say, "Abraham rejoiced to see my day: and he saw it, and was glad" (John 8:56).

(2) *Abraham's discovery confirmed by revelation*

"Even as David also describeth the blessedness of the man, unto whom God imputeth righteousness without works."

"Saying, Blessed are they whose iniquities are forgiven, and whose sins are covered."

"Blessed is the man to whom the Lord will not impute sin" (vs. 6-8).

Paul here makes a quotation from David in Psalm 32.

The forensic sense of justification is here fully manifested. The great doctrine of imputation which lies at the heart of justification is declared. The believer or "the blessed man" of Psalm 32 has his sins not placed to his account. They are not imputed to him, that is they are not reckoned to be his at all. Instead, righteousness apart from works is reckoned to be his. His justification is by faith alone. The wondrous act which bring this about is the Lord's.

In the court-room the believing sinner is not merely acquitted but justified, given a standing as if he had never sinned. Man may pardon but only God can justify.

[This section completed on the twenty-first day of imprisonment: Wednesday, 10th August, 1966]

(b) *Abraham's Designation - Blessedness in faith alone*

"Cometh this blessedness then upon the circumcision only, or upon the uncircumcision also? for we say that faith was reckoned to Abraham for righteousness".

"How was it then reckoned? When he was in circumcision or in uncircumcision? Not in circumcision but in uncircumcision."

"And he received the sign of circumcision, a seal of the righteousness of the faith which he had yet being uncircumcised: that he might be the father of all them that believe, though they be not circumcised; that righteousness might be imputed unto them also":

"And the father of circumcision to them that are not of the circumcision only, but who also walk in the steps of that faith of our father Abraham which he had being yet uncircumcised" (vs. 9-12).

Justified Abraham is here designated, "not in circumcision but in uncircumcision". The timing of his circumcision is important. If he had been justified by works then the divine declaration of his justification would have come after and not before his circumcision. He would have been reckoned just, "in his circumcision, and not without it".

Such, however, is not the case.

In Genesis chapter fifteen we read the divine declaration of Abraham's justification, "And he believed in the Lord; and He counted it to him for righteousness" (v. 6).

In the following chapter we have the birth of Ishmael and an important matter is mentioned, the age of Abraham, "And Abraham was fourscore and six years old, when Hagar bore Ishmael" (Gen. 16:16).

The next chapter, chapter seventeen, commences with Abraham's age being again recorded. It tells of the divine command of circumcision and both in verse one and verse twenty-four the age of Abraham is noted. Abraham is now "ninety years old and nine". So for thirteen years in circumcision he walked in the knowledge and enjoyment of justification without works. He knew the blessedness of faith alone. In this blessedness of faith alone he became the possessor of a unique fatherhood, the father of all them that believe, (v. 11), and the father of circumcision, (v. 12).

Moreover circumcision is a seal not of something to be attained by works, but of something to be obtained as a gift i.e. "the righteousness of faith which he had being yet uncircumcised", (v. 11).

Therefore Abraham's blessedness was in faith alone, thus he is designated "not in circumcision, but in uncircumcision" (v. 10).

(c) *Abraham's Destiny - Sovereignty of faith alone*

"For the promise that he should be the heir of the world, was not to Abraham, or to his seed, through the law, but through the righteousness of faith."

"For if they which are of the law be heirs, faith is made void, and the promise made of none effect."

"Because the law worketh wrath: for where no law is, there is no transgression."

"Therefore it is of faith, that it might be by grace; to the end the promise might be sure to all the seed; not to that only which is of the law, but to that also which is of the faith of Abraham; who is the father of us all."

"(As it is written, I have made thee a father of many nations,) before Him whom he believed, even God, who quickeneth the dead, and calleth those things which be not as though they were" (vs. 13-17).

(1) *The Sovereignty of Abraham himself*

Abraham's sovereignty is here clearly stated. He is appointed "heir of the world" (v. 13), and "a father of many nations" (v. 17).

Now the promise of God which assured Abraham of these things was given before his circumcision. Remembering that the command of circumcision was given in Genesis chapter seventeen verse ten let us turn to verses four and five of the same chapter.

Before, not after the command to be circumcised, God changed his name to Abraham for said God "a father of many nations I have made thee". This was not of works but "of faith that it might be of grace" (Rom. 4:16).

There are no "thou shalts" in these verses but rather the "I wills" of Jehovah and the "Thou shalt be's" of grace.

Notice the five "I wills" (five in scripture is the number of grace).

(1) *"I will* make thee exceedingly fruitful" (Gen. 17:6).

(2) *"I will* make nations of thee" (v. 6).

(3) *"I will* establish my covenant for an everlasting covenant" (v. 7).

(4) *"I will* give unto thee the land" (v. 8).

(5) *"I will* be their God" *(v. 8).*

Here is Abraham's Destiny - Sovereignty by faith alone.

(2) *the Sovereignty of Abraham's seed*

Abraham's seed are not merely those of the Jewish nation, the circumcised. He is not the father of one nation but as his name signifies of many nations.

Now the seed of Abraham who are to enjoy sovereignty are not heirs of the law for then God's promise would be made of none effect, (v. 13). They are rather heirs by the righteousness of faith without the law.

Their sovereignty is sure for it depends not on their works but on the Word of the God that cannot lie.

"Therefore it is of faith, that it might be by grace; to the end the promise might be sure to all the seed; not to that only which is of the law, but to all that also which is of the faith of Abraham; who is the father of us all" (v. 16).

It is sovereignty by faith alone.

(d) *Abraham's Determination - Triumph by faith alone*

"Who against hope believed in hope, that he might become the father of many nations; according to that which was spoken, so shall thy seed be."

"And being not weak in faith, he considered not his own body now dead, when he was about an hundred years old, neither yet the deadness of Sarah's womb."

"He staggered not at the promise of God through unbelief; but was strong in faith, giving glory to God."

"And being fully persuaded that, what He had promised, he was able also to perform."

"And therefore it was imputed to him for righteousness" (vs. 18-22).

(1) *His determination overcame spiritual weakness*

"Who against hope believed in hope." He was called Abraham the father of many nations yet he had not one son by his only wife, Sarah. How spiritual weakness must at many times have overwhelmed him!

"Who against hope believed in hope". What depths of spiritual agonies are sounded here!

"Who against hope believed in hope". What spiritual struggles are wrapped up in this sentence of six words!

"Who against hope believed in hope". What spiritual victories do these words chronicle!

(2) *His determination overcame physical weakness*

"He considered not his own body now dead, when he was about one hundred years old, neither yet the deadness of Sarah's womb" - v. 19.

The Genesis narrative is worthy of consideration here.

Genesis 17, vs. 15-17 reads:

"And God said unto Abraham, As for Sarai thy wife, thou shalt not call her name Sarai, but Sarah shall her name be."

"And I will bless her, and give thee a son also of her: yea, I will bless her, and she shall be a mother of nations; kings of people shall be of her."

"Then Abraham fell upon his face, and laughed, and said in his heart, shall a child be born unto him that is an hundred years old? and shall Sarah that is ninety years old bear?"

Genesis 18, vs. 9-15 read:

"And they said unto him, Where is Sarah, thy wife? And he said, behold, in the tent."

"And He said, I will certainly return unto thee according to the time of life: and, lo, Sarah, thy wife shall have a son."

"And Sarah heard it in the tent door, which was behind him."

"Now Abraham and Sarah were old and well stricken in age; and it ceased to be with Sarah after the manner of women."

"Therefore Sarah laughed within herself, saying, After I am waxed old shall I have pleasure, my lord being old also?"

"And the Lord said unto Abraham, Wherefore did Sarah laugh, saying, shall I of a surety bear a child, which am old?"

"Is anything too hard for the Lord? At the time appointed I will return unto thee, according to the time of life, and Sarah shall have a son".

"Then Sarah denied, saying, I laughed not; for she was afraid. And He said, Nay; but thou didst laugh."

Sarah physically speaking could not be a mother. "It ceased to be with Sarah after the manner of women" and Abraham physically speaking could not be a father, "his own body (sexually) was dead" yet he "staggered not at the promise of God through unbelief but was strong in faith giving glory to God", v. 20. Herein is the triumph of faith alone.

> *Faith, mighty faith the promise sees,*
> *And looks to God alone;*
> *Laughs at impossibilities*
> *And cries, it shall be done.*

2   THE CONCLUSION OF THE CASE

"Now it was not written for his sake alone, that it was imputed to him":

"But for us also, to whom it shall be imputed, if we believe on Him that raised up Jesus our Lord from the dead. Who was delivered for our offences, and was raised again for our justification." Vs. 23-25.

Hebrews chapter eleven, verses 17-19 should be carefully noted in this connection.

"By faith Abraham, when he was tried, offered up Isaac; and he that had received the promises offered up his only begotten son; Of whom it was said, That in Isaac shall thy seed be called!"

"Accounting that God was able to raise him up, even from the dead; from whence also he received him in a figure."

The giving back of Isaac to Abraham from the altar of death was a type of the resurrection of our Lord, God's only begotten Son. In Isaac sacrificed on the altar and then restored to him by divine intervention, faith saw the death and resurrection of our Saviour. We have already noted the scripture "Abraham rejoiced to see my day" (i.e. the day of Christ's resurrection); "he saw it and was glad" (John 8:56). It should also be noted that each time the words "it was imputed unto him for righteousness" are spoken of Abraham they are spoken of his faith in his promised seed, which is Christ.

"Now to Abraham and his seed were the promises made. He saith not, and to seeds, as of many; but as of one, and to thy seed, which is Christ" (Gal. 3:16).

The conclusion of the case is then that Abraham was justified by faith alone through "a righteousness without the law" imputed to him according to grace and that we too, by the same grace, can have this righteousness imputed to us.

[This section completed on the twenty-second day of imprisonment:
Thursday, 11th August, 1966]

In this conclusion we have, in a nutshell, the great doctrines, which in the following chapters, Paul expounds.

(1) *The provision* of this "righteousness without the law".

"Who was delivered for our offences."

(The word "for has the meaning "because of".)

Christ was delivered because of our offences. His spotless life offered up in the death of the Cross provides a perfect righteousness for His people.

(2) *The Proof* of this "righteousness without the law."

"And was raised for our justification" (i.e. because of our justification).

The mighty debt being paid and perfect righteousness without the law provided, Christ must rise from the dead. Justice could no longer imprison him. The resurrection is the mighty proof of our justification.

(3) *The Provider* of this "righteousness without the law".

"Him that raised our Lord Jesus Christ from the dead."

Yes, with the old Puritan we can say,

> *"God the Father thought it,*
> *God the Son bought it,*
> *God the Spirit wrought it,*
> *The Devil fought it,*
> *but, Glory to God,*
> *I got it."[1]*

(4) *The Procurement* of this "righteousness without the law".

"if we believe".

Faith and faith alone procures this imputed righteousness for the sinner.

[This section completed on the twenty-third day of imprisonment:
Friday, 12th August, 1966]

Footnotes

1. The resurrection of our Lord Jesus Christ is ascribed to each member of the Holy Trinity; to God the Father (Gal. 1:1), to God the Son (John 10:18), to God the Spirit (Rom. 1:4). (See comment on this verse.)

5 The therefore of our justification
and the wherefore of our identification

THIS CHAPTER HAS two great sections. The first section, verses one to eleven, commencing with the word "therefore expounds "the therefore of our Justification and the second section, verses twelve to twenty-one, commencing with the word "wherefore" expounds "the wherefore of our Identification".

1   THE THEREFORE OF OUR JUSTIFICATION, vs 1-11

These verses uniquely unfold seven characteristics of "the righteousness without the law" which justifies the believer. Paul is speaking to believers and thus he uses the word "we" which is the personal pronoun in the first person plural. He does not use the third person "they". For he wishes to identify himself with the believers and to speak from experience.

(a) *The Source of our Justification*
"For scarcely for a righteous man will one die; yet peradventure for a good man some would even dare to die."

But God commendeth His love toward us, in that, while we were yet sinners, Christ died for us," vs 7 and 8.

How is man, sinful, polluted, vile, unworthy, to be justified without the works of the law? He is hell-bent and hopelessly and totally depraved. There seems only hell, eternal hell, for such as he. Yes, but in the darkness of man's depravity there ariseth the heavenly light (II Cor. 4:6). Over the humanly speaking impossibilities write the golden words "But God".

God, the Father Himself, is the source of our justification. It comes to us in the tremendous current of His everlasting love. The wise woman of Tekoah spoke eternal truth when she said to David, "For we must needs die, and are as water spilt on the ground, which cannot be gathered up again; neither doth God respect any person, yet doth He devise means, that His banished be not expelled from Him" (II Sam. 14:14). The word used in verse 8 for "commend" occurs only in two other places in the epistle, in chapter 3, verse 5, "But if our unrighteousness commend the righteousness of God" and in chapter 16, verse 1, "I commend unto you Phebe". In chapter 3:5 the commendation is by way of contrast. The righteousness of God contrasted with the unrighteousness of man commends itself.

In chapter 16:1 the commendation is by way of character. Phebe is recommended for what she is of herself. "For," says Paul, "she has been a succourer of many" (chapter 16:2).

God's own love, the source of our justification, is commended both by contrast and by character. "But God commendeth His love (lit. His own love) towards us, in that (1) (By way of contrast) while we were yet sinners (2) (By way of character) Christ died for us."

The contrast of God's love with the background of the hellish blackness of our loathsomeness, commends the heavenly brightness of God's love.

"For scarcely for a righteous man will one die; yet peradventure for a good man some would even dare to die.

"But God commendeth His love towards us, in that, while we were YET SINNERS" God's love is thus commended by contrast.

But God's love is also commended by its character. "Christ died for us". When God loved He loved the world. When God gave He gave His Son (John 3:16).

God's love is thus commended by its character.

(b) *The Secret of our Justification*

"for when we were yet without strength in due time, Christ died for the ungodly", v. 6. This is the central verse of these eleven verses, five verses come before it and five verses come after it. Verse 6 is the centre, the very heart of this particular passage and in it the heart-secret of justification without works is discovered.

How can God be just and yet justify the sinners? How can unholy man be reconciled to his holy Maker? How can eternal mercy in holiness rejoice against eternal justice? How can the citizens of the City of Destruction become by right the citizens of Mount Zion? How can Paradise Lost be Paradise regained?

This verse reveals the secret.

"When we were yet without strength", unable ourselves to do anything, "in due time Christ died for the ungodly".

The word "for" has the meaning "in behalf of". The word "ungodly" is a strong word. It is used by Peter to describe the sinners of Noah's day. "Bringing in the flood upon the world of the ungodly" (II Pet. 2:5). It literally means the irreverent, the impious. On their behalf Christ died. We have here the great doctrine of substitution, the innocent dying for the guilty; the just for the unjust; the righteous for the unrighteous; the law maker and the law keeper for the law breaker.

Christ died in due time. Having Fulfilled the law to its last tittle and jot, then in due time, when His hour had come[1] Christ offered Himself without spot to God on behalf of the ungodly.

The Christ who lived for me, died for me.

> *Upon a life I did not live,*
> *Upon a death I did not die,*
> *Another's life, another's death,*
> *I stake my all eternally.*

His life was in order to His life-giving. He was born in order to bleed. His obedience was in order to His offering, He was made under the law to redeem those that were under the law by magnifying the law and making it honourable (Gal. 4:4 and 5: Isa. 42:21).

In verse 9 we read we are "justified by His blood". Now the basic idea of blood is not death and impotence but life and the potency. This is illustrated in the modern blood transfusion. The blood is the life "for the life of the flesh is in the blood" (Lev 17:11).

Christ's life in the flesh, a life which perfectly kept the law, must be made available for us. By death, His life in the flesh, His blood, was released and its potency thus made available for His people.

It was not spilled blood, that would be an accident, it was shed blood, for this is ATONEMENT.

His blood not only provides cleansing but clothing. The sins are remitted and the sinner is robed. Through the blood there is not only remission of sins but admission to heaven.

"The blood of Jesus Christ, His Son, cleanseth us from all sin," - that's our cleansing; and we are made "the righteousness of God in Him"; - that's our clothing (I John 1:7, and II Cor. 5:21).

The righteousness of Christ is reckoned to be ours; it is imputed to us.

Thus we are cleansed and thus we are clothed and stand justified (just as if we had never sinned) before our Maker.

> *Jesus, Thy blood and righteousness*
> *My beauty are, my glorious dress;*
> *Midst flaming worlds, in these arrayed,*
> *With joy shall I lift up my head.*
>
> *When, from the dust of death, I rise*
> *To take my mansion in the skies;*
> *E'en then shall this be all my plea -*
> *Jesus hath lived and died for me.*
>
> *Bold shall I stand in that great day,*
> *For who ought to my charge shall lay,*
> *While, thro' thy blood, absolved I am*
> *From sin's tremendous curse and shame.*
>
> *This spotless robe the same appears*
> *When ruined nature sinks in years,*
> *No age can change its glorious hue,*
> *The robe of Christ is ever new.*
>
> *Oh, let the dead now hear thy voice!*
> *Bid, Lord, thy banished ones rejoice;*
> *Their beauty this, their glorious dress,*
> *Jesus, Thy blood and righteousness.*

HALLELUJAH TO THE LAMB!

[This section completed on the twenty-fifth day of imprisonment:
Lord's Day, 14th August, 1966]

(c) *The Seal of our Justification*

"Because the love of God is shed abroad in our hearts by the Holy Ghost which is given unto us", v. 5.

The source of our justification is God the Father. The secret of our justification is God the Son.

The seal of our justification is God the Holy Spirit. In these verses we have God in Trinity and Trinity in Unity working out the justification of the sinner.

Justification is sealed in the believer's heart

"in our hearts" v. 5.

Justification is heart work as opposed to head work. We must believe, not with the head, but with the heart. "Shalt believe in thine heart" is the divine command (Rom. 10: 9).

Justification is a spiritual work as opposed to a sacramental work. It is heart-washing by the blood of Jesus as opposed to baptism by water. Men are saved not by sacraments officiated on them by the hands of their fellows but by the work of the Spirit of God within their hearts. It is not by the shedding abroad of liquid on their bodies but by the shedding abroad of love in their hearts that men know they are justified.

Justification is an inward change of standing before God as opposed to an outward change of standing before men.

By justification the righteousness of Jesus is reckoned to be ours and this is sealed in our hearts in a change of standing before God. Once we stood in condemnation, now we stand in justification. Once we stood overshadowed by God's wrath, now we stand overwhelmed by God's love. Once we stood a rebel in God's sight, now we stand reconciled by God's Son. Our outward standing before men is the same, our inward standing before God is transformed. Man looks on the outward appearance but God looks on the heart.

Justification is sealed in the believer's heart by the Holy Ghost.

"By the Holy Ghost."

The indwelling person of God the Holy ghost is the seal of our justification. The seal is not a blessing but the Blesser Himself. The Holy Spirit is the seal of our justification as well as of our sanctification and redemption.

"God who hath also sealed us and given the earnest of the Spirit in our hearts" (II Cor. 1:21 and 22).

"Ye were sealed with that Holy Spirit of promise which is the earnest of our inheritance" (Eph. 1:13 and 14).

"The Holy Spirit of God, whereby ye are sealed unto the day of redemption" (Eph. 4:30).

The Holy Ghost is the pledge that in the coming day when eternal destinies shall be everlastingly decided no condemnation shall fall on me. Justified now in time, the Holy Spirit Himself is the earnest that in the day of judgment I shall be completely and eternally declared righteous before heaven, earth and hell. Hallelujah!

Justification is sealed in the believer's heart by the Holy Ghost which is given unto us.

"Which is given unto us".

The earnest in a contract is the token payment of the full amount and the pledge that the terms of the contract shall be completely honoured. Now God has given to us such a pledge in the person of His Spirit. The Holy Spirit is the token gift of the whole covenant transaction and the pledge that the full terms of the contract shall be completely honoured. The Spirit is given unto us. He is gifted unto us. "For the gifts and calling of God are without repentance" (Rom. 11:29).

The Holy Spirit thus given to us is the token now privately in our spirits that we are justified (Rom. 8:16) and the pledge that in that great day of judgment we shall be publicly declared eternally righteous through the righteousness of Christ alone. What grace! What a gift! What glory!

> *O Breath from far Eternity,*
> *Breathe o'er my soul's unfertile land,*
> *So shall the pine and myrtle tree,*
> *Spring up amidst the desert sand;*
> *And where thy living water flows,*
> *My heart shall blossom as the rose.*

[This section completed on the twenty-seventh day of imprisonment: Tuesday, 16th August, 1966]

(d) *The Science of Our Justification*

"Therefore being justified *by faith*", v. 1.

The science or knowledge of justification by the imputed righteousness of Christ is faith. By faith the soul closes with Christ freely offered in the Gospel. By faith that soul cries out, "I want no other"; "I will trust no other"; "I will depend on no other"; "I will see no other"; "I will hear no other"; "I will cling to no other"; "I will cry to no other"; "I will have no other but Jesus Christ and Him alone for my salvation". The old preacher was right when he took an acrostic on faith had preached thus:

F = Forsaking
A = All
I = I
T = Trust
H = Him.

Forsaking all I trust Him.

Faith has two empty hands and those two hands can only be filled with Christ alone.

Faith has two swift feet and those two feet lead to Christ alone.

Faith has two open eyes and those two eyes look to Christ alone.

Faith has two listening ears and those two ears hearken to Christ alone.

Faith is abandonment to Jesus. It wants nothing but Christ. It asks for nothing but Christ. It trusts nothing but Christ. It is content with nothing but Christ. It will cling to nothing but Christ. Its life is bound up in Christ and Christ alone. It is lovesickness for the Saviour and it unceasingly cries, "Though He slay me yet will I trust Him".

Faith is not however a mad, rash, unthinking abandonment. Faith is an abandonment begotten of knowledge. "Faith cometh by hearing, and hearing by the Word of God" (Rom. 10:17). The soul has heard of Christ by the word of God preached or read. The soul sees in Him and in Him alone all that he requires, cleansing for his sinfulness; clothing for his nakedness; health for his sickness; life for his lifelessness; hope for his hopelessness, and home for his homelessness. With the knowledge of his own exceeding impotence and of the exceeding sufficiency of Christ, faith enables the soul to exclaim:

"Thou, O Christ, art all I want
More than all in Thee I find."

Yes, and faith further enables the soul to experience all that it longs for in a blessed eternal union with the Saviour. Faith is the eternal link which unites the soul everlastingly to the Lord. It is the marriage ring which seals the soul in heavenly matrimony with the celestial bridegroom.

"O Faith that quickened me in death,
I owe my inward life to thee.
By thee God's Son is mine indeed,
And has supplied my every need,
By Blood at Calvary."

[This section completed on Thursday, 18th August, twenty-ninth day of imprisonment]

(e) *The Signs of our Justification*

"Therefore being justified by faith, we have peace with God through our Lord Jesus Christ."

"By whom also we have access by faith into this grace wherein we stand, and rejoice in hope of the glory of God.

"And not only so, but we glory in tribulations also; knowing that tribulation worketh patience, and patience experience; and experience, hope and hope maketh not ashamed", vs. 1-5.

The signs of our justification are seen in -

1. Our State
2. Our Standing
3. Our Steps

(1) *Our State*

"Therefore being justified by faith we have peace with God through our Lord Jesus Christ", v. 1.

The first sign of justification is the realisation of the new state which we have before God. Our state in sin was one of rebellion against God. We were rebels alienated from the life of God by the darkness of our hearts. We lifted up hands in sinful anarchy against God's laws. We used, nay rather abused our lips, to blaspheme God's throne. Our hearts were seed-beds of rebellion against their Maker.

But our state has now been gloriously changed. We have peace - What rest!

With God - What reconciliation!

Through our Lord Jesus Christ - What reassurance!

What rest!

"The wicked are like the troubled sea, when it cannot rest, whose waters cast up mire and dirt. There is no peace, saith my God, to the wicked" (Isa. 57:20). What a terrible state is the state of being without peace.

Without peace of conscience. O the calamity of the one who carries his own accuser in his breast!

Without peace of mind. O the curse of a mind set adrift on the mad sea of imagination and ambition!

Without peace of soul. O the consternation of a soul without rest, tossed to and fro on the uncontrollable currents of its own passions and habits!

What a rest is that which delivers us from it all.

The previous verse to the one just quoted from Isaiah gives the answer.

"Peace, peace to him that is far off, and to him that is near, saith the Lord; and I will heal him" (Isa. 57:19).

What rest to possess peace of conscience.

"Peace, perfect peace, in this dark world of sin.
The blood of Jesus whispers peace within!"

What rest to know peace of mind.

Every thought brought into captivity to the mind of Christ (II Cor 10:5), and the mind renewed continually by the Holy Ghost (Eph 4:23).

What rest to experience peace of soul.

To have eternal calm in the very depths of one's being, that is rest indeed. Peace, eternal peace is one of the signs of our justification.

[This section completed on the thirtieth day of imprisonment: Friday, 19th August, 1966]

What reconciliation!

"With God."

Justification brings peace *with God*.

He that is afar off is brought nigh. He that was a rebel is now reconciled. He that was a child of hell is now a child of heaven. A new relationship has been established. The separating wall between the sinner and God is removed. Christ has purged our sins and as our representative has sat down on the right hand of the Majesty on high (Heb. 1:3).

"Now therefore ye are no more strangers and foreigners, but fellow-citizens with the saints, and of the household of God; and are built upon the foundation of the apostles and prophets, Jesus Christ Himself being the chief cornerstone" (Eph. 2:19 and 20).

Peace with God, eternal peace with God is one of the signs of our justification.

What reassurance!

"through our Lord Jesus Christ".

What reassurance this brings to the believing soul. The peace with God is through our Lord Jesus Christ. Herein is the nature of this peace revealed. It partakes not of the mutability of earth; it is clothed with the immutibility of heaven. We have peace through our Lord Jesus Christ for He Himself, in all the glory of His Ineffable Deity, in all the grace of His Impeccable Humanity and in all the power of His Infinite Blood-shedding, is our peace (Eph. 2:14).

Notice the full titles of the Saviour are here given, our Lord Jesus Christ. These full titles occur three times in the chapter. They set out the work of grace in the believer's life.

(1) *The Reception of Grace*

"peace with God through our Lord Jesus Christ", v. 1.

(2) *The Rejoicing of Grace*

"joy in God through our Lord Jesus Christ."

(3) *The Reign of Grace*

"grace reign through righteousness unto eternal life by Jesus Christ our Lord, v. 21.

In considering these titles we must ever remember:

He is exalted Lord

"Wherefore God also hath highly exalted Him, and given Him a name which is above every name; and that the name of Jesus every knee should bow, of things in heaven, and things in earth and things under the earth; that every tongue should confess that Jesus Christ is Lord, to the glory of God the Father" (Philippians 2:9-11).

He is called Jesus

"Thou shalt call His name Jesus: for He shall save His people from their sins" (Matt. 1:21).

He is anointed Christ

"God anointed Jesus of Nazareth with the Holy Ghost and with power" (Acts 10:38). (Christ lit. means anointed.)

He is mine

"Our Lord Jesus Christ.

"Ten thousand charms around Him shine;

But best of all I know He's mine."

Peace through our Lord Jesus Christ. Eternal Peace through our Lord Jesus Christ is one of the signs of our justification.

(2) *Our Standing*

"By whom also we have access by faith into this grace wherein we stand, and rejoice in hope of the glory of God", v. 2.

The realisation of our new standing before God is another sign of our justification. There are three great facts here concerning our position by justification.

(i) We have access - The entrance of our standing.

(ii) We stand - The experience of our standing.

(iii) We rejoice in hope - The expectancy of our standing.

The Entrance of our Standing

"By whom we have access by faith."

"Whom" refers to our Lord Jesus Christ in verse 1.

"By" means lit. "through".

So Christ is the entrance - "I am the door". "I am the way". Hence we could read this clause thus, "Through our Lord Jesus Christ we have a leading into, by faith, this grace wherein we stand, etc." By faith we appropriate Christ as our entrance through which we come into our new standing with God. The entrance of our standing is Christ.

The Experience of our Standing

"The grace wherein we stand."

Grace is unmerited favour. The experience of our standing is the experience of the place of unmerited favour and that place is the person of Christ. He is "this grace wherein we stand". The entrance of our standing is Christ and the experience of our standing is Christ. Yes and:

> *"I know no safer stand,*
> *Not e'en where glory dwelleth*
> *In Immanuel's land."*

I stand in Christ.

The Expectancy of our Standing

"and rejoice in hope of the glory of God." Our expectancy causes us to rejoice. It is a joyful expectancy. Its joy is begotten of a great hope, which hope we have as an anchor of the soul both sure and steadfast (Heb. 6:19). It is the hope of the glory of God, that is the hope of perceiving and partaking in the full manifestation of that glory. The glory of God is only known in the face of Jesus Christ; "the knowledge of the glory of God in the face of Jesus Christ". Our expectancy is Christ; a face to face eternal contemplation of our Lord.

> *Face to face! O blissful moment!*
> *Face to face - to see and know;*
> *Face to face with my Redeemer,*
> *Jesus Christ who loves me so.*

> *Face to face shall I behold Him.*
> *Far beyond the starry sky,*
> *Face to face in all His glory*
> *I shall see Him by and by.*

The entrance of our standing is Christ; the experience of our standing is Christ and the expectancy of our standing is Christ. The realisation of these three blessed relationships with Christ is the second sign of our justification.

(3) *Our Steps*

"And not only so, but we glory in tribulations also; knowing that tribulation worketh patience; and patience, experience; and experience, hope: and hope maketh not ashamed", vs. 3-5. In the previous chapter we have a reference to those who "walk in the steps of that faith of our father Abraham" (Rom. 4:12).

The taking and the testing of these steps are signs of our justification.

First, tribulation

Tribulation here means pressure and affliction. This affliction comes because of the just man's walk of righteousness in the world. It is not the affliction that results from our sin, such affliction we deserve. It is the affliction that results from our not sinning, such affliction we must endure.

When Abraham first stepped out to obey God tribulation was his portion.

Tribulation came to him through *the Folly of the Family*. His father Terah uncalled by God journeyed with him to Haran and dwelt there, thus preventing Abraham from entering into Canaan. Through this folly of the family, affliction came to Abraham as he took the first steps of faith. Yes, and we who walk in the steps of that faith shall also know tribulation through the folly of the family. A man's foes shall be they of his own household (Matt. 10:36). To step out in faith and by faith means stepping out into tribulation in the family.

Then Abraham experienced tribulation through *the Burden of Business*.

Lot fought with Abraham over the burden of business and Abraham knew deep anguish. Business in this crooked world, yes prosperity in business, brings a burden, a burden which, in the path of faith, causes tribulation.

Again Abraham had tribulation through *the Battle of the Backslider*. Chapter 14 of Genesis records the anxiety of Abraham for the backslider, Lot, and the battle which he fought to save him.

What affliction Abraham had when Lot still persisted in staying in Sodom! The heart cry of Abraham for Sodom in Genesis 18 sounds the depths of his affliction in the battle for the backslider. The justified man will have tribulations, pressures, afflictions in the battle for the backslider. To be wounded in the house of one's friend is part of the price of that battle.

Further, Abraham had tribulation from *the Ways of the World*.

Sarah his wife was a very beautiful woman. Wherever Abraham journeyed men set lustful eyes upon her. At the beginning of his journey the fact of his wife's beauty and the ways of the world brought him tribulation. His pact with Sarah to deny her marriage to him was a vain attempt to placate the ways of the world. Sarah also seemed to acquiesce too readily in the scheme. The way of the world evidently pleased her. Genesis 12 should be read in this connection. What tribulation resulted to Abraham in Egypt! Even when Sarah was old she was still a very attractive woman. Abimelech, the King of Gerah, took her to be his wife when told by Abraham the half truth that she was his sister. Sarah again consented readily and what tribulation must have resulted to Abraham. The heathen king actually reproved her. See Genesis 20 and especially verse 16. The justified man will have tribulation from the ways of the world. Moreover, Abraham had tribulation from *the Wiles of Women*. Sarah, not content to wait God's time to obtain the promised son God's way, encouraged Abraham to take for his second wife, Hagar, her maid. When Hagar conceived the son which Sarah wanted, then Sarah, the instigator of the whole business, sought to blame her husband and even the Lord. See Genesis 16:4-6. Hagar and Sarah fought and then Ishmael and Isaac fought. The wiles of women brought old Abraham much affliction. The depths of this affliction is sounded in the eleventh verse of the twenty-first chapter of Genesis.

Afflictions will come to the justified through the wiles of women. Such tribulations mark the steps of the righteous man.

Christ warned, "In the world ye shall have tribulation" (John 16:33). The apostle Paul affirmed "We must through much tribulation enter into the Kingdom of God" (Acts 14:22).

The steps of the justified then will be manifested with such tribulations. Tribulations resulting from (1) the folly of the family; (2) the burden of business;

(3) the battle of the backslider; (4) the ways of the world; (5) the wiles of the women.

[This section completed on Tuesday, 23rd August, 1966, thirty-fourth day of imprisonment]

Second, patience
The word here translated patience has the meaning of endurance, continuance. There is another Greek word translated patience which has the meaning of forbearance, long-suffering. See James 5:10 and Matthew 18:26. But the word here is endurance.

The sign of justification is that of one enduring and continuing amidst tribulation. Tribulation will blight a professor of justification but will bless a possessor of justification.

The word translated "worketh" is a strong word meaning lit. to work down, to work thoroughly - a finished work.

Patience in the sense of endurance, continuance, is seen clearly in the life of Abraham, in the steps of whose precious faith all the justified walk. Abraham's tribulations wrought out within him patience, an enduring to the end, a continuance in the path of faith. The Scriptures tell us that, "after he had patiently endured, he obtained the promise" (Hebrews 6:15).

The tribulation which came to him through the folly of the family worked within him continuance in *the pilgrimage of faith*. When the folly of hindering Terah ceased with his death, Abraham immediately continued his pilgrimage to Canaan. "And into the land of Canaan they came" (Gen. 12:5. See Heb 11:15 and 16).

The tribulation which came to him through the burden of business worked within him continuance in *the provision of faith*. He trusted God to provide for him before he arrived in Canaan and now when Lot had taken to himself the best of the land he continued in the provision of faith. Nor did his continuance go unrewarded. "And the Lord said unto Abram, after that Lot was separated from him, Lift up now thine eyes, and look from the place where thou art northward, and southward, and eastward, and westward. For all the land which thou seest, to thee will I give it, and to thy seed forever. And I will make thy seed as the dust of the earth: so that if a man can number the dust of the earth, then shall thy seed also be numbered. Arise, walk through the land in the length of it and in the breadth of it: for I will give it unto thee" (Gen. 13:14-17).

The tribulation which came to him through the battle of the backslider worked within him continuance in *the prayer of faith*. His prayer for Lot was answered for, because of it, God could not bring destruction on Sodom until Lot was safe (Gen. 19:22).

The tribulation which came to him through the ways of the world worked within him continuance in *the path of faith*. He tarried not in Egypt (Gen. 13) nor in Gerah (Gen. 20). He continued as a sojourner and pilgrim (Heb. 11:9, 10).

The tribulation which came to him through the wiles of women worked within him continuance in *the promise of faith*. He believed God even after the birth of Ishmael and in due time received the promise in the birth of Isaac.

Further signs of justification are the steps of patience in the pilgrimage of faith.

**[This section completed on thirty-fifth day of imprisonment:
Wednesday, 24th August, 1966]**

Third, experience

This word "experience means "proof". It is translated thus in II Corinthians 2:9, Corinthians 13:3, Philippians 2:22. Tribulation worketh endurance and endurance proof. The reality of justification is shown by its public proving of God.

In his continuance in the pilgrimage of faith, Abraham proved *the reality of God's call*. Stephen tells us, "The God of glory appeared unto our father Abraham, when he was in Mesopotamia, before he dwelt in Charran, and said unto him, Get thee out of thy country, and from thy kindred, and come into the land which I shall shew thee. Then came he out of the land of the Chaldeans, and dwelt in Charran; and from thence, when his father was dead, he removed him into this land, wherein ye now dwell" (Acts 7:2-4).

Immediately Abraham continued in the pilgrimage of faith and came into Canaan God appeared to him again. He had a further experience of the proof of God. Patience worketh experience!

In his continuance in the provision of faith, Abraham proved *the inexhaustibility of God's care*. Lot sought to take care of himself by the choice of the fertile plain of Jordan (Gen. 13:10). Abraham proved the inexhaustibility of God's care for when Lot died he had lost everything, even his own purity and his daughters' virtue (Gen. 19) while when Abraham died he had gained everything especially the promise. Herein he had a further proof of experience of God. Patience worketh experience!

In his continuance in the prayer of faith, Abraham proved *the intensity of God's compassion*. Every request Abraham made for Sodom, God granted. It was only when Abraham stopped asking that God stopped granting. Abraham proved that day the intensity of God's compassion (Gen. 18:23-33). He had a further proof or experience of God. Patience worketh experience!

In his continuance in the path of faith, Abraham proved *the effectuality of God's control*. The over-ruling by God of Sarah's reception by Pharaoh in Egypt (Gen. 12) and by Abimelech in Gerah (Gen. 20) proved to Abraham the effectuality of God's control.

The honour of the mother of the promised seed could have been stained with the blackest adultery but for God's control. Thereby Abraham had a further experience or proof of God. Patience worketh experience!

These proofs are signs of justification by faith alone.

Fourth, hope

Hope means expectation, and experience worketh expectation.

The proof of the reality of God's call worked within Abraham the hope or expectation of *the provision of the seed*. Since God, having brought him into the promised land, he expected God to fulfil the rest of His covenant (Gen. 12:2 and 3). Experience worketh hope!

The proof of the inexhaustibility of God's care worked within Abraham the hope or expectation of *the prosperity of the seed*. He expected God to prosper the seed of promise. This was his great hope. Experience worketh hope!

The proof of the intensity of God's compassion worked within Abraham the hope or expectation of *the potency of the seed*. God manifested the power which He had delegated to Abraham and to his seed after him when He said, "Shall I hide from Abraham that thing which I do; seeing that Abraham shall surely become a great and mighty nation, and all the nations of the earth shall be blessed in him?"

"For I know him, that he will command his children and his household after him, and they shall keep the way of the Lord, to do justice and judgment; that the Lord may bring upon Abraham that which He hath spoken of him" (Gen. 18:17-19). As Abraham proved the intensity of God's compassion in the potency of the prayer of faith so he expected that his seed would be a power with God on earth. He surely hoped and expected that the covenant promise that all nations of the earth would be blessed through his seed would be gloriously fulfilled. Experience worketh hope!

The proof of the effectuality of God's control worked in Abraham the hope or expectation of *the protection of the seed*. The God who protected Sarah from dishonour he expected would similarly protect her seed. Experience worketh hope!

The proof of the immutability of God's character worked in Abraham the hope or expectation of *the preservation of the seed*. He expected God to preserve the seed alive even in death.

"By faith Abraham, when he was tried, offered up Isaac; and he that had received the promises offered up his only begotten son, of whom it was said, That in Isaac shall thy seed be called: Accounting that God was able to raise him up, even from the dead; from whence also he received him in a figure" (Heb. 11:17-19). Experience worketh hope! This hope is yet another sign of our justification.

THE STEPS OF THAT FAITH OF OUR FATHER ABRAHAM
Romans 4:12
Tribulation worketh patience and patience experience and experience hope.

TRIBULATION *means: pressure afflictions.*	PATIENCE *means: endurance continuance.*	EXPERIENCE *means: proof.*	HOPE *means: expectation.*
1. The folly of the family.	1. The pilgrimage of faith.	1. The reality of God's call.	1. The provision of the seed.
2. The burden of business.	2. The provision of faith.	2. The inexhaustibility of God's care.	2. The prosperity of the seed.
3. The battle of the backslider.	3. The prayer of faith.	3. The intensity of God's compassion.	3. The potency of the seed.
4. The ways of the world.	4. The path of faith.	4. The effectuality of God's control.	4. The protection of the seed.
5. The wiles of women.	5. The promise of faith.	5. The immutability of God's character.	5. The preservation of the seed.

(f) *The Security of our justification*

"Much more then, being now justified by His blood, we shall be saved from wrath through Him. For if when we were enemies, we were reconciled to

God by the death of His Son, much more, being reconciled, we shall be saved by His life", vs. 9, 20.

Justification is an irreversible act. The justified soul is secure eternally. His eternal salvation is settled. The "much more" argument of Paul cannot be gainsaid. Our past, present and future are all connected in this apostolic logic.

(1) *Our Past*

"we were enemies"

Once again Paul stresses our dreadful position in sin. We were the enemies of God. We rebelled against Him. We cursed Him. We fought against Him. We broke His laws. We trampled on His love.

What did God do? Did He damn us? Nay verily, He commended His love toward us in that while we were yet sinners Christ died for us. When we deserved nothing but wrath He bestowed on us nothing but grace. When there was nothing to commend us, God gave His son to save us. This is grace indeed!

(2) *Our Present*

"being now justified by His blood".

"we were reconciled by the death of His Son".

Our sins are cleansed away in the precious blood of the Lamb and we are declared righteous in God's sight. The rebellion is no more for we are now reconciled to God. Note, this was all done for us when we were enemies. What shall God not do for us now that we are cleansed on the terms of fellowship with Him?

(3) *Our Future*

"We shall be saved from wrath through Him."

"We shall be saved by His life."

If God has commended His love toward us while we were yet sinners; if He has sent His Son to die for us while we were His enemies and if we have been reconciled and cleansed when we deserved to go to hell, much more, now that we are His children, will God not save us from coming wrath? Yes, and the grand reason for this confidence of completed salvation is Christ's life. We shall be saved by His life.

What life is this? His life now in heaven? No, I do not think so. The answer is found in what it saves us from. We are not saved from wrath by His life now in Heaven. It is His life and death on earth which saves us from wrath to come. In order to get to heaven we require: (1) cleansing from our sin and (2) a positive righteousness to fit us for God's presence. Cleansing alone would not make us meet for heaven. We must be clothed and being clothed we shall not be found naked. Now on the cross Christ not only died for my sin being made sin, but He offered Himself without spot to God (II Cor. 5:21, Heb. 9:14). In His blood there is not only power to cleanse but power to clothe.[2] He parted with His life in the flesh at the cross and His righteous life in His blood, for the life of the flesh is in the blood.

Now that we are cleansed from our sins much more shall we be clothed and declared to be positively righteous by Christ's life and thus saved from wrath through Him.[3] That is Paul's argument.[4] Such is the security of our justification.

(g) *The Song of our Justification*

"And not only so, but we joy in God through our Lord Jesus Christ, by whom we have now received the atonement", v.11.

Paul concludes this section of "The Therefore of Our Justification" with the doxology of the justified, the song of justification.

(1) *Its tune is joyful*

"joy in God"

It is the joyful tune of salvation's new song which is put in the mouth of the justified (Ps. 40:3).

It shall burst forth some day in eternal crescendo when all who have learned its melody unite to give it the celestial rendering.

"And I heard a voice from Heaven, as the voice of many waters, and as the voice of a great thunder: and I heard the voice of harpers harping with their harps: And they sung as it were a new song before the throne, and before the four beasts, and the elders: and no man could learn that song but the hundred and forty and four thousand, which were redeemed from the earth" (Rev. 14: 2, 3).

(2) *Its theme is Jesus*

"Through our Lord Jesus Christ, by whom we have now received the atonement."

Its theme is *the person of Christ* - our Lord Jesus Christ. We view Him in His deity, He is Lord. We view Him in His humanity, He is Jesus. We view Him in His mediatorial capacity, He is Christ, anointed prophet, priest and king for His people.

Its theme is *the work of Christ* - the atonement. The word "atonement is "reconciliation". Atonement meaning "to cover" occurs only in the Old Testament. The New Testament word is reconciliation and means to make a thorough change. This is the only place in the Authorised Version of the New Testament where it is translated "atonement". In all other places it is translated "reconciliation".

The work of Christ was to change us thoroughly. For this He suffered on the Cross. The Cross is the Transforming Cross.

Its theme is *the grace of Christ* - "by whom we have received".

All we have, we have received. The grace of Christ is the foundation, fabric and finish of our salvation. We are what we are by grace alone. Christ's free unmerited, undeserved favour is the theme of our song.

"And when He had taken the book, the four beasts and the four and twenty elders fell down before the Lamb, having everyone of them harps, and golden vials full of odours, which are the prayers of saints. And they sung a new song, saying, Thou art worthy to take the book, and to open the seals thereof: for Thou wast slain, and hast redeemed us to God by Thy blood out of every kindred, and tongue, and people, and nation; And hast made us unto our God, kings and priests: and we shall reign on the earth" (Rev. 5:8-10).

[This section completed on the thirty-seventh day of imprisonment: Friday, 26th August, 1966]

2   THE WHEREFORE OF OUR IDENTIFICATION, vs. 12-21

It was Martin Luther the Reformer who said, "There are but two men, Adam and Christ, and all other men hang at their girdles".

These two men; the first and the last Adam (I Cor. 15:45), the first man of the earth, earthy, the second man the Lord from heaven (I Cor. 15: 47); and the position of those identified with them, are the theme of these verses.

(a) *Identification with both Adam and Christ through Physical Association*

"By one man (Adam) sin", v. 12.

"grace, which is by one man, Jesus Christ", v. 15.

We are identified with Adam through physical association. He is our first parent and physically we have been begotten from his loins. We are his offspring. He was of the earth, earthy; and we bear the image of the earthy (I Cor. 15:49). We are fashioned of his clay and are partakers of his flesh and blood.

Our identification with Adam is through physical association. We are also identified with Jesus Christ through physical association. He, who was eternally God, miraculously, by the Virgin Birth, became man. By becoming man He did not cease to be God but rather united the two distinct natures, Deity and Humanity, in His one person forever.

"The Word was made flesh, and dwelt among us" (John 1:14).

"That which was from the beginning, which we have heard, which we have seen with our eyes, which we have looked upon, and our hands have handled, of the Word of Life" (I John 1:1).

"God sent forth His Son, made of woman, made under the law" (Gal. 4:4).

In Luke's Gospel the genealogy of the Lord Jesus Christ is traced right back to Adam (Luke 3:23-38).

"Forasmuch then as the children are partakers of flesh and blood, He also Himself likewise took part of the same" (Heb. 2:14).

"For verily He took not on Him the nature of angels; but He took on Him the seed of Abraham" (Heb. 2:16). The word "redeemer" in the Old Testament is "goel the kinsman redeemer. See Ruth 3:9. So we can say of Him, "He is flesh of our flesh and bone of our bone."

Our identification with Christ is through physical association.

(b) *Identification with both Adam and Christ through Federal Representation*

(Adam) "who is the figure of Him that was to come", v. 14.

"Therefore as by the offence of one judgment came upon all men to condemnation; even so by the righteousness of one the free gift came upon all men, unto justification of life. For as by one man's disobedience many were made sinners, so by the obedience of one shall many be made righteous", vs. 18, 19.

Adam is a figure or type of Him that was to come, that is our Lord Jesus Christ, for Adam is the representative man of the old creation, its fount and spring, as Christ is the representative man, the fount and spring, of the new creation. Adam is our federal head as sinners. Christ is our federal head as saints. We hang at their girdles, as Luther said.

We are identified with Adam through federal representation. He is our federal head naturally. He entered into covenant with God not only for himself but for his posterity to obey God's commandment. He recognised his federal headship for he discharged its responsibility by instructing his wife, Eve, in the nature of God's law and of the penalty resulting from its violation. This should be carefully noted. In Genesis 2:16 and 17 we have God's commandment: "And the Lord God commanded man, saying, Of every tree of the garden thou mayest freely eat: but of the tree of knowledge of good and evil, thou shalt not eat of it; for in the day thou eatest thereof thou shalt surely die"

Now these words were spoken to Adam before Eve was made. Eve did not hear the command yet she was bound by it for Adam was not only her husband but her federal head. Eve herself recognised the federal headship of her husband and her obligation, because of his covenant with God, strictly to keep the commandment. Hence her reply to the serpent,

"We may eat of the fruit of the trees of the garden; but of the fruit of the tree which is in the midst of the garden, God hath said, Ye shall not eat of it, neither shall ye touch it, lest ye die" (Gen. 3: 2, 3).

Now Adam disobeyed the law of God by the one offence of eating the forbidden fruit and not only sinned himself but sinned for and on behalf of all his posterity by natural generation, as their federal representative. So the Original Sin, which originated all our sins and sinnings, was committed. When Adam sinned we were identified with his sin because he was our federal head. He not only acted for himself but he acted for us as our representative. We were in his loins when he fell and we fell in him and through him.

Our identification with Adam is through federal representation.

We are also identified with Jesus Christ through federal representation. He is our federal head spiritually. As Adam entered into a covenant with God not only for himself but for his posterity so Jesus Christ entered into a covenant with God not only for Himself but for His people. This is the covenant of grace and of redemption. Obedience to the law was demanded by God of Adam, he disobeyed by one offence and its result was condemnation. The offence of verse 18 is linked with the disobedience of verse 19.

Obedience to the law was demanded by God of Jesus Christ. He was made under the law, that is, He willingly subjected Himself to its rule. "Think not", He said, "I am come to destroy the law, or the prophets, I am not come to destroy, but to fulfil" (Matt. 5:17). He came to magnify the law and make it honourable. It has been disgraced by disobedience. He came to grace it with obedience. Notice the righteousness of verse 18 is linked with the obedience of verse 19, and results in the making of many righteous.

The word righteous in verse 18 means accomplished righteousness, that is, the fulfilment of the righteous requirements of the law. This is what Christ's obedience was. By obedience He fulfilled the righteous requirements of the law. This obedience had its climax in the cross for He "became obedient unto death, even the death of the cross" (Phil. 2:8).

By His obedience we are constituted righteous. He fulfilled the law for us. We were in His loins when He accomplished its very jot and tittle. He is made unto us wisdom, righteousness, sanctification and redemption (I Cor. 1:30). He is Jehovah - Tsidkenu, "The Lord our righteousness" (Jer. 23:6; 33:16).

> *When free grace awoke me,*
> *By light from on high,*
> *Then legal fears shook me,*
> *I trembled to die;*
> *No refuge, no safety,*
> *In self could I see,*
> *"Jehovah Tsidkenu"*
> *My Saviour must be.*

Our identification with Christ is through federal representation.

***[This section completed on the thirty-ninth day of imprisonment:
Lord's Day, 28th August, 1966]***

(c) *Identification with both Adam and Christ through Judicial Participation*

"Wherefore, as by one man sin entered into the world, and death by sin; and so death passed upon all men, for that all have sinned: (For until the law sin was in the world: but sin is not imputed when there is no law. Nevertheless death reigned from Adam to Moses, even over them that had not sinned after the similitude of Adam's transgression, who is the figure of Him that was to come. But not as the offence, so also is the free gift. For if through the offence of one many be dead, much more the grace of God, and the gift by grace, which is by one man, Jesus Christ, hath abounded unto many. And not as it was by one that sinned, so is the gift; for the judgment was by one to condemnation, but the free gift is of many offences unto justification. For if by one man's offence death reigned by one; much more they which receive abundance of grace and of the gift of righteousness shall reign in life by one, Jesus Christ)", vs. 12-17.

We are identified with Adam through judicial participation. We are not only partakers of his sin but also of the sentence passed upon him because of that sin. Judgment has come upon us all. Condemnation is our portion. Death is our penalty.

(1) We participate in Adam's *nakedness before God*.

"And the eyes of them both (Adam and Eve) were opened, and they knew that they were naked; and they sewed fig leaves together, and made themselves aprons. And they heard the voice of the Lord God walking in the garden in the cool of the day: and Adam and his wife hid themselves from the presence of the Lord God amongst the tree of the garden. And the Lord God called unto Adam, and said unto him. Where art thou? And he said, I heard Thy voice in the garden, and I was afraid, because I was naked; and I hid myself" (Gen. 3:7-10).

Like Adam we are naked before God. The glory has departed and as partakers in Adam's sin we participate in Adam's sentence. With Job we can but cry "Naked came I out of my mother's womb, and naked shall I return thither" (Job 1:21). It is evident that Job is referring to the womb of mother nature. He certainly did not think he would return to his own mother's womb. Naturally we are naked both in birth and in death.

(2) We participate in Adam's *hardness towards God.*

Sinful man wants to get away from God. He seeks a hiding place from God's face. Sin has hardened his heart. When he comes face to face with God, the hardness of his heart is manifested by his language of hated against God. He seeks to place the responsibility for sin upon the thrice holy Jehovah. "The woman whom Thou gavest to be with me, she gave me of the tree, and I did eat" (Gen. 3:12). Not the woman thou gavest me but thou gavest to be with me. What hardness sin begets!

Yes, and all of us have partaken of this hardness against God. "The heart is deceitful above all things, and desperately wicked; who can know it?" (Jer. 17: 9).

Sin is itsown detective ("Be sure your sin will find you out" Num. 32:23), and it carries its own judgment with it. "The way of transgressors is hard" (Prov. 13:15).

(3) We participate in Adam's *darkness from God*

The sentence passed on Adam brought *darkness on his lodging*. Eden's garden with its brightness was no longer his home. "The Lord God sent him forth from the garden of Eden, to till the ground from whence he was taken. So he drove out the man" (Gen. 3: 23, 24). He became a pilgrim in the world with darkness upon his every lodging place the darkness of distance from God.

The sentence also brought *darkness on his land*. The very land which he walked upon and possessed for his living partook of the shadow of the curse. "Cursed is the ground for thy sake" (Gen. 3:17). Darkness was upon his land, the darkness of desolation.

The sentence further brought *darkness on his labours*. No lasting joy or prosperity could ever be his through his labours. "In sorrow shalt thou eat of it all the days of thy life; thorns also and thistles shall it bring forth to thee; and thou shalt eat the herb of the field; in the sweat of thy face shalt thou eat bread", such was the sentence of God (Gen. 3:17-19). Darkness overshadowed all his labours, the darkness of disappointment and distress. The sentence finally brought *darkness on his life*. "Till thou return unto the ground; for out of it wast thou taken; for dust thou art, and unto dust shalt thou return" (Gen. 3:19).

Adam was doomed to die, the shadow of the grave was ever about him. Darkness overhung his whole life, the darkness of death. The sentence was, "Thou shalt surely die" (Gen. 2: 17).

Through judicial participation we are identified with Adam in his nakedness before God, his hardness toward God and his darkness from God. The sentence passed on him was also passed on us. We participate in the penalty and partake of its curse.

We are also identified with Jesus Christ through judicial participation. As we have participated judicially in the blight of the life and disobedience of Adam so we have participated judicially in the blessing of the life and obedience of Jesus Christ. By the standard of the law Adam was guilty, full of sin and evil. By the standard of the law, the Lord Jesus was glorious, full of grace and truth.

The sentence of the law on Adam we have participated in, hence our nakedness before God, our hardness toward God and our darkness from God.

The findings of the law on Jesus Christ we have also participated in, hence our righteousness before God, our blessedness toward God and our brightness from God. We participated in Christ's *righteousness before God*. His righteousness, that is, his accomplishment of the righteous requirements of the law is not only His but ours. Through the grace of God, this righteousness which is "the gift by grace has abounded to us" v. 15. Judicially it is reckoned to be ours.

John Bunyan[5] says:

"Here is a righteousness that Christ as God, has no need of, for He is God without it; here is a righteousness that Christ as man has no need of to make Him so, here is a righteousness that Christ as God-man has no need of, for He is perfectly so without it. Here, then, is a righteousness that Christ, as God, as man, as God-man, has no need of with reference to Himself, and therefore He can spare it; a justifying righteousness, that He for Himself, wanteth not, and therefore He giveth it away; hence it is called, "the gift of righteousness".

We participate in Christ's *blessedness toward God*. God surveyed His Incarnate Son as He was on earth and bore Him this testimony, "This is my beloved Son, in whom I am well pleased" (Matt. 3:17).

Christ in stating the purpose of his great excursion from heaven to earth said, "Lo, I come (in the volume of the book it is written of Me) to do Thy will, O

God" (Heb. 10:7). In this blessedness toward God, which is Christ's we participate. This is the abundance of grace which we have received, v. 17.

We participate in Christ's *brightness from God*.

We participate in the brightness of *Christ's lodging*. His lodge, His tabernacle, His temple is the church, which is His body, the fullness of Him that filleth all in all (Eph. 1:23). Like the Israelites in Egypt we participate in God's light; amidst the darkness we have light in our dwellings (Exoc. 10:23). We also participate in the brightness of *Christ's land*. We walk spiritually through Immanuel's land and there the brightness of Christ's transforming grace shines forth in all the lustre of heavenly glory. Yes, and we shall possess eternally the land of the heavenly Canaan of which Christ is the light thereof.

"And the city hath no need of sun, neither of the moon, to shine in it: for the glory of God did lighten it, and the Lamb is the light thereof. And the nations of them that are saved shall walk in the light of it" (Rev. 21:23, 24).

We further participate in the brightness of *Christ's labours*. What brightness shines over the labours of Christ for the lost. Yes, and we are participants in those labours. As we are His joy and crown so are those to us, whom we, through partaking of His labours, have won to Him (Phil. 4:1). The brightness of His labours rests upon us.

Finally we participate in the brightness of *Christ's life*.

Christ is the true light which coming into the world lighteth every man (John 1:9).

"I am the light of the world" said Jesus. Yet again He saith "Ye are the light of the world" (John 8:12), (Matt. 5:14). We are to participate in the brightness of His life for if we follow Him we shall have, He Himself declares, the light of life (John 8:12). Our identification with Christ is through judicial participation.

(d) *Identification with Christ alone through Eternal Exaltation*

"Moreover the law entered, that the offence might abound. But where sin abounded, grace did much more abound; that as sin hath reigned unto death, even so might grace reign through the righteousness unto eternal life by Jesus Christ our Lord", vs. 20, 21.

The contrast and comparison of Adam with Christ finishes at verse 19. In these last two verses we are identified with Christ alone through spiritual exaltation.

Archibald G Brown, one of CH Spurgeon's students and after Spurgeon's son, Thomas, pastor at The Metropolitan Tabernacle, called this chapter the chapter of the five kings. In verses 14 and 17, there is King Death reigning. In verse 21 there is King Sin reigning. In verse 21 there is King Grace reigning. In verse 17 King Saint reigns and all through the chapter it is implied that King Jesus reigns.

King Sin ruled and reigned over us. The firstborn of Sin, King Death, also wielded his desolating sceptre over our lost soul. Sin abounded and through the law we learned bitterly its dominion and curse. The eternal death cell was to be our everlasting destiny. But Jesus came, Praise His name, and identified us with Himself in His eternal exaltation.

(1) *Eternal Exaltation in Life*

Ephesians chapter one speaks of Christ's exaltation in life from the dead. Chapter two tells us of our identification with Him in that exaltation in life. "Even when we were dead in sins, hath quickened us together with Christ, and hath raised us up together, and made us sit together in heavenly places in Christ Jesus. That in the ages to come He might shew the exceeding riches of His grace in His kindness toward us through Christ Jesus" (Eph 2:5-7).

This is what is meant when it says "unto eternal life by Jesus Christ our Lord", v. 21. This is our exaltation in life, or "reigning in life by one Jesus Christ", v. 17.

(2) *Eternal Exaltation by Grace*

Where sin abounded grace superabounded. King Grace challenged King Sin for our dominion and King Grace won the battle. King Sin is dethroned; his reign is past; "He *hath* reigned", saith the text. King Grace has triumphed, grace reigns. By free, unmerited, undeserved favour we are what we are. Notice the repetition of the word "gift" in the passage.

"the free gift"
"the gift by grace"   } v 15.
"the gift"
"the free gift"   } v 16.
"the gift of righteousness", v. 17.

Five is the number of grace in scripture and here the gift is mentioned five times. (In verse 18 it is in italics which means it is not in the original.)

(3) *Eternal Exaltation through Righteousness*

We are eternally exalted through righteousness. He arose righteously from the dead, the law had no claims on Him. Justice was satisfied by the blood-   shedding on the tree. Robed in His righteousness we rise in Him to eternal exaltation.

We were:

One when He died,
One when He arose.
One when He triumphed,
O'er all His foes.
One in heaven when He took His seat,
And all heaven rejoiced o'er hell's defeat.

We are identified with Christ alone in His eternal exaltation.

[This section completed on the fortieth day of imprisonment:
Monday, 29th August, 1966]

Footnotes

1. In the Gospel of John the Lord Jesus Christ makes frequent reference to His death as the culminating act of His ministry on earth.
    To His mother at the wedding feast He said, "Mine hour is not yet come" (John 2:4).
    When His enemies in their hatred were going to destroy Him they could not fulfil their wicked design "Because His hour was not yet come" (John 7:30; 8:20).
    When the Greeks requested an audience He said, "The hour is come, that the Son of Man should be glorified" (John 12: 23, 27).
    The Passover discourses were introduced with the statement that Jesus "knew that His hour had come" (John 13:1).
    The same discourses contain the passage "The hour cometh, yea, is now come that ye shall be scattered" (John 16:32).
    Finally in the great High Priestly prayer, He said, "Father, the hour is come" (John 17:1).
2. This truth is beautifully expressed in the lines of Dr Horatius Bonar's great communion hymn. "Mine is the sin, but Thine the righteousness; Mine is the guilt, but Thine the cleansing blood: Here is my robe, my refuge and my peace - Thy blood, Thy righteousness, O Lord my God."
3. The man without the wedding garment was cast out into wrath (see Matt. 22:11-14).
4. John Bunyan gives this very clear and distinct account of being saved by Christ's life in Part Two of his *Pilgrim's Progress* when he records the speech of Greatheart to Christina after they leave the House of the Interpreter. We would commend this to our readers.
5. One of my fellow prisoners, Rev Ivan Foster, has a copy of John Bunyan's Works with him and I am being greatly refreshed by reading again the Immortal Dream, *The Pilgrim's Progress*. The above is from one of the wonderful discourses of Greatheart in Part II of the work.

6 The science of our *emancipation*

CHAPTER FIVE DEALS with our standing; chapter six deals with our state. Chapter five explains our position; chapter six explains our condition. Chapter five expounds the act of justification; chapter six expounds the work of sanctification. In chapter five we have freedom from sin practically. Chapter six is the chapter of the science or knowledge of our emancipation. Its key is found in verse 14, "Sin shall not have dominion over you".

In verses 1-10 we have The Conception of Sanctification explained; in verses 11 and 12 we have The Crucifixion of Self exhorted; in verses 13-23 we have The Consecration of Service experienced.

1. THE CONCEPTION OF SANCTIFICATION EXPLAINED, vs. 1-10

(a) *The Logic of our Sanctification*

"What shall we say then? Shall we continue in sin, that grace may abound? God forbid. How shall we that are dead to sin, live any longer therein?" verses 1, 2.

Sanctification is the logical outcome of our justification through Christ and our identification with Christ.

Our twofold relationship with sin cannot logically continue, (1) living in sin, "live any longer therein" - v. 2, and (2) continuing in sin, "continue in sin" - v. 1.

Living in sin, or life in sin, has to do with the principle of sin.

Continuing in sin has to do with the practice of sin. When the cross comes into operation, and "we are dead to sin" - v. 2, the principle of sin is dealt with. When grace comes into operation, "grace may abound" v. 1, the practice of sin is dealt with. Herein is the logic of our sanctification.

(b) *The law of our Sanctification*

"Know ye not, that so many of us as were baptised into Jesus Christ were baptised into His death? Therefore we are buried with Him by baptism into death; that like as Christ was raised up from the dead by the glory of the father, even so we also should walk in newness of life. For if we have been planted together in the likeness of His death, we shall also be in the likeness of His resurrection" vs. 3-5.

The law of sanctification is the law of the baptism and the planting.

The baptism here, I believe, is the spiritual baptism of which baptism with water is the symbol. It is the inward spiritual work of which water baptism is the outward visible sign.

Baptism with water does not put anybody into Christ but the spiritual baptism, of which water baptism is the symbol, does do so. The baptism here referred to is the one spiritual baptism of Ephesians 5:5 and spoken of by the Apostle in I Corinthians 12:13 thus:

"For by one spirit are we all baptised into one body." Now the basic idea both of the substance, spiritual baptism, and the symbol, water baptism, is union. Israel were "all baptised" unto Moses in the cloud and in the sea (I Cor. 10:2) - union with Moses. "for as many of you as have been baptised into Christ have put on Christ. There is neither Jew nor Greek, there is neither bond nor free, there is neither male nor female; for ye are all one in Christ Jesus" (Gal. 3:27, 28) - union with Christ.

[This section completed on forty-first day of imprisonment: Tuesday, 30th August, 1966]

Union with Christ is the principle of our sanctification. It is this principle which has sanctified us (i.e. made us what we are positionally) and it is the operation of this principle which sanctifies us (i.e. makes us what we are practically).

Now we have two great truths in these verses, the truth of baptism and the truth of planting. In these the law of our sanctification is revealed.

The baptism, the act, the principle of our sanctification. The planting, a work suggesting growing, setting forth the operation of the principle, or the practice of sanctification.

Baptism - The Principle

"Know ye not, that so many of us as were baptised into Jesus Christ were baptised into His death? Therefore we are buried with him by baptism into death; that like as Christ was raised up from the dead by the glory of the Father, even so we also should walk in newness of life", vs. 3-4.

Verse four begins with one of Paul's great "therefores". This ushers in his conclusion to the previous verse. Our walking in newness of life, which is indeed sanctification, rests upon the principle of vital union with Christ in His Cross work. This union is brought about by a mighty baptism which puts us into Christ, which buries us with Him, and which raises us up with Him by the glory of the Father. This mighty baptism is the spiritual baptism, as we already noted, of which water baptism is the outward and visible sign. First of all then we must consider the great truth that our sanctification was accomplished at the cross and by the tomb and that Christ by His death and resurrection is our sanctification.

(1) *Sanctification Accomplished For Us*

The basic meaning of the word, to sanctify, is, to separate, to set apart. From this we learn the truth of a separation from and a setting apart to.

We are separated from,

(a) The World - from its love.
(b) The Flesh - from its lust.
(c) The Devil from his law.

We are set apart to be,

(a) holy
(b) without blemish } Ephesians 1:4
(c) in love

Now our sanctification is ascribed to all three persons in the Godhead and to the word of God.

(a) *God the Father*: "to them that are sanctified by God the Father", Jude verse one. Sanctification is the work of God the Father in the decreeing of it, its purpose and planning.

(b) *God the Son*: "Wherefore Jesus also, that he mighty sanctify the people with His own Blood" (Heb. 13:12). Sanctification is the work of God the Son in *the determining* of it, that is, it's settling and accomplishing.

(c) *God the Holy Ghost*: "Sanctified by the Holy ghost" (Rom. 15:16). Sanctification is the work of God the Holy Ghost in *the directing* of it, that is, its imparting and purifying.

(d) *The Word of God*: "Sanctify them through Thy truth: Thy Word is truth" (John 17:17).

Sanctification is the work of the Word of God, in *the demonstrating* of it, that is, its effecting and out-working.

*[This section completed on the forty-fifth day of imprisonment:
Saturday, 3rd September, 1966]*

**N.B. I am now half-way through my sentence. Praise the Lord for His
presence and power (Heb. 12:3).**

Sanctification, the work of God the Son, in its settling and accomplishment is the great truth declared in these verses. Christ accomplished or settled our sanctification for us by His death on the cross, by His burial in the earth and by His rising again from the dead. The Lord Jesus refers to His death, burial and resurrection as a baptism.

"But I have a baptism to be baptised with; and how am I straitened until it be accomplished!" (Luke 12:50). Our sanctification was accomplished for us in the mighty baptism of His Cross work. The Scriptures make this abundantly clear.

"Then He said, Lo, I am come to do thy will, O God. He taketh away the first that he may establish the second. By the which will we are *sanctified* through the offering of the body of Jesus Christ once for all" (Heb. 10:9, 10).

"For by one offering He hath perfected for ever them that are *sanctified*" (Heb. 10:14).

"Christ also loved the church, and gave Himself for it; that He might *sanctify* and cleanse it " (Eph. 5:25, 26).

"Jesus also, that He might *sanctify* the people with His own blood" (Heb. 13:12).

In these last two scriptures, the great objective of Christ's sufferings is shown to be the sanctification of His people - the church.

The first two scriptures declare that Christ accomplished this great objective on the cross. His people are sanctified; sanctification for them has been settled by Christ in His mediatorial offering upon the tree. Their sanctification is a fact, accomplished by the act of Christ. Christ crucified, buried, and risen again, is their sanctification (I Cor. 1:30).

(2) *Sanctification accomplished in us*

The sanctification accomplished for us must also be accomplished in us. Christ's death, burial and resurrection, the accomplishment of sanctification for us, we must partake of if sanctification is to be accomplished in us. Only by vital union with Christ in His death, burial, and resurrection can this be realised. This vital union, as we have already noticed, is the principle of sanctification.

Now as our sanctification was accomplished for us by a baptism, the baptism of our Lord's sufferings, so our sanctification is accomplished in us by a Baptism, the baptism in the Spirit into the one body (I Cor. 12: 12). This spiritual baptism vitally unites us to Christ, and makes us partakers in the accomplishment of sanctification. By it sanctification, accomplished for us by Christ, is accomplished in us with Christ. By our baptism we share in His baptism. Two scriptures are worthy of close study in this connection.

Christ's Baptism	*Our Baptism*
"Can ye drink of the cup that I drink of? and be baptised with baptism that I am baptised with? And they said unto Him, We can. And Jesus said unto them, Ye shall indeed drink of the cup that I drink of; and with the baptism that I am baptised withal shall ye be baptised" (Mark 10:38-39).	For by one Spirit are we all baptised unto one body, whether we be Jews or Gentiles, whether we be bond or free; and have been all made to drink into one spirit (I Cor. 12:13).

These scriptures demonstrate how by our baptism we share Christ's baptism and thus partake with Him of the one cup. The baptism and the drinking of the cup, both for Christ and us, are linked together. Our baptism makes us one with Christ.

It is an eternal act which vitally unites us to Christ, the living Head, constitutes us members of His body and so identifies us with His glorious self that we actively share in His death and experimentally partake of His resurrection. Thus our sanctification is accomplished in us.

Birth is the family truth. We are born again and become members of His family.

Baptism is the church truth. We are baptised and become members of His body. Both take place simultaneously when Christ is received as Lord and Saviour. The Christ received is Christ our sanctification.

This is plainly taught in the Word of God. Believers are sanctified. Sanctification is accomplished in them. They possess vital union with Christ which is the principle of sanctification.

There was no more carnal nor sinful church than that of Corinth yet Paul speaks of them as those, "That *are sanctified* in Christ Jesus" (I Cor. 1:2). This expression deserves attention. It deals, of course, with our standing or sanctification accomplished in us. This sanctification is accomplished because we are *"in Christ Jesus"*, it was the mighty spiritual baptism which put us into Christ.

"For ye are all the children of God by faith in Christ Jesus" (the family truth).

"for as many of you as have been baptised into Christ have put on Christ" (the church truth). "There is neither Jew nor Greek, there is neither bond nor free, there is neither male nor female; for ye are all one *in Christ* Jesus " (Gal. 3:26-28).

Of the same Corinthian people Paul wrote, "But ye are washed, but *ye are sanctified*" (I Cor. 6:11).

In Hebrews we read "For both He that sanctifieth and they who *are sanctified* are all of one; for which cause He is not ashamed to call them brethren" (Heb. 2: 11).

These scriptures all refer to sanctification accomplished in us through the spiritual baptism which vitally joins us to Christ.

(2) Planting - The Operation of the Principle

"For if we have been planted together in the likeness of His death, we shall be also in the likeness of His resurrection", v. 5.

Now baptism suggests an act. Baptism in water is not a work but an act. It is not continued but is final. So is the spiritual baptism of which it is an outward visible sign. Planting however suggests growth - a work. The previous verse on baptism brought before us two acts intimately connected together, both of which are final.

(1) Christ's baptism resulting in sanctification accomplished for us.

(2) Our baptism resulting in sanctification accomplished in us.

Sanctification must also be accomplished through us. This is the great truth taught in this verse. The planting, inferring the taking root, the growing and the bearing fruit, set forth the work of

(3) *Sanctification accomplished through us*

The principle of sanctification in operation is the practice of sanctification. This practice is of course a work. It is the working out through us, that is through our whole being and life, the sanctification already accomplished for us and in us.

It is to this sanctification, accomplished through us, that the scriptures exhort.

"This is the will of God, even your *sanctification*, that ye should abstain from fornication" (I Thess 4:3). "That they also might be *sanctified* through the truth" (John 17:10).

"*Sanctify* them through Thy truth; Thy word is truth" (John 17:17).

"And the very God of peace *sanctify* you wholly" (I Thess. 5:23).

Now this work is set forth in our text in the truth of planting. The principle is death, burial, and resurrection, the operation of which is seen in the planting, the taking root and the springing up. An Old Testament text will bring out beautifully for us the operation of this principle.

"And the remnant that is escaped of the house of Judah, shall yet again take root downward and bear fruit upward" (II Kings 19:30).

In the planting there must be the downwards of rooting before there can be the upwards of shooting. The deeper the root, the stronger the shoot. Yes, and our planting is a planting in the likeness of His death. What were the depths of His death?

Now we cannot and will not go down into death by ourselves. We cry out against death; we want to live. But the word is planted together (this is its only occurrence in the New Testament), for Christ takes us down into death. We are planted together with the conqueror of death, that corn of wheat, with life which can never die in its kernel. In the planting we decrease; we partake of self-extinguishing darkness; we die. The corn of wheat must fall into the ground and die if it would bear much fruit (John 12:24).

We not only take root downward however, but we bear fruit upward. We die and behold we live! We die daily to live daily. We go down continually to rise up continually. We decrease constantly to increase constantly. The principle is in operation and thus sanctification is accomplished through us. The old catechism is right, "Sanctification is a work of the Holy Spirit whereby we are enabled more and more to die unto sin and to live unto righteousness".

The law of our sanctification then is the law of our baptism and planting.

[This section completed on 4th September, 1966, forty-sixth day of imprisonment]

(c) *The Liberty of our Sanctification*

"Knowing this, that our old man is crucified with Him, that the body of sin might be destroyed, that henceforth we should not serve sin. For he that is dead is freed from sin", vs. 6, 7.

Our sanctification and emancipation results from knowledge. Knowledge is power. "Ye shall know the truth, and the truth shall make you free" (John 8:32). This knowledge is threefold. (1) Knowledge of an historical fact, (2) Knowledge of a doctrinal truth and (3) knowledge of a legal maxim.

(1) *The Historical Fact*

"Our old man is crucified with Christ".

The expression "old man" occurs only in two other places in the New Testament.

"That ye put off concerning the former conversation the old man, which is corrupt according to the deceitful lusts" (Eph. 4: 22). Here we have plainly stated *The corruption of the old man*.

"Corrupt according to the deceitful lusts".

The conversation of the old man

"The former conversation or manner of life". This conversation or manner of life of the old man is described in the previous verses. "Having the understanding darkened, being alienated from the life of God through the ignorance that is in them, because of the blindness of their heart. Who being past feeling have given themselves over unto lasciviousness, to work all uncleanness with greediness" (Eph. 4:18, 19).

Note it is the deeds of the old man, the conversation or manner of life which we are called to put off.

The other scripture in which this expression "old man" occurs confirms this.

"Lie not one to another, seeing ye have put off the old man with his deeds" (Col. 3:9).

Here we have

The character of the old man

He is a liar and the words of the Lord Jesus are most appropriate here.

"Ye are of your father the devil, and the lusts of your father ye will do. He was a murderer from the beginning, and abode not in the truth, because there is no truth in him. When he speaketh a lie, he speaketh of his own; for he is a liar, and the father of it" (John 8:44). The old man is that which we have received from Adam. It is the old Adam in us, our corrupt sinful nature. No person is able to put off the old man in the absolute sense, nor is there any spiritual exhortation commanding us to do so. These scriptures of exhortation, as we have seen, deal with the deeds of the old man but not with the old man himself. Failure to know the truth on this vital issue has led to much distress, despair and depression amongst many sincere people of God. It is the Cross of Christ and not the will or resolution of the believer which deals with the old man.

This scripture declares a fact which is completely outside our persons and powers, "Our old man is (lit. was) crucified with Christ". We have nothing whatsoever to do with it. This is the dynamic work of Christ on the cross. The great historical fact is this, that along with Christ on the Cross our old man was crucified. God did not send the old man to hospital to be cured but to the Cross to be crucified. The old man is not dealt with by the believer's confession, nor by the believer's contrition, nor by the believer's consecration; the old man has been dealt with by the Cross. As the lofty Sisera bowed, fell, lay down, and fell down dead (Judges 5:27), so the old man, the tyrant of the race, was slain at Calvary's cross. This is a fact, an historical fact, a scriptural fact, and a blessed fact. In its knowledge there is emancipation, the liberty of our sanctification.

(2) *The Doctrinal Truth*

"That the body of sin might be destroyed, and henceforth we should not serve sin."

"Our old man has been crucified with Christ"; that is history.

"That the body of sin might be destroyed, that hence forth we should not serve sin"; that is doctrine.

"The body of sin", "the body of this death" (Rom. 7:24), and "the body of the sins of the flesh" (Col. 2:11), are expressions.

"That the body of sin might be destroyed," that henceforth we should not serve sin". We come to expound chapter seven. The words "might be destroyed" deserve careful attention. What is this destruction? Is the old man in us extinct? Is the old nature annihilated or eradicated? Now there are many Greek words translated in our New Testament by the word, "destroy". There is a word which means to kill (see Matt. 2:13); a word which means to mar utterly (see Rev. 8:9); a word which means to destroy utterly (see Acts 3:23); a word which means to take down (see Acts 13:19); a word which means to take down (see Acts 6:14); a word which means to loose (see I John 3:8); a word which means to lay waste (see Acts 9:21); and a word which means to corrupt (see I Cor. 3:17). All these different words are translated in these texts by the word destroy. Now it is none of these words which is used here. The word used here means lit., "to make of none effect, to make inoperative, to render powerless, to rob of its power to rule". A look at another text where it occurs will help to bring out the meaning. "That through death He (Our Lord Jesus Christ) might destroy him that had the power of death, that is, the devil" (Heb. 2:14).

Now the devil is not extinct nor is he annihilated. But at the Cross he was rendered powerless, his right to rule was taken from him, he was dethroned. The seed of the woman bruised his head (Gen. 3:15). We must learn this great doctrine that as with the devil so with our old nature, both by the cross are rendered powerless. If the old man rules he is a usurper for he has been dethroned. We should not therefore serve sin, is the proclamation of our text. Sin's kingdom is smashed and it has no rightful hold upon us.

In the knowledge of this doctrinal truth, there is emancipation, the liberty of our sanctification.

(3) *The Legal Maxim*

"For he that is dead is freed from sin", v. 7. In verse 1 of the next chapter we read that the law hath dominion over a man only so long as he liveth. When death comes the rule of law ceaseth. Now not only is the old man crucified, but I am also crucified and have become a partaker of Christ's death, vs. 3, 4 (Gal. 2:20). The law of sin cannot any more rule over me for he that is dead is freed from sin. In the knowledge of this legal maxim there is emancipation, the liberty of our sanctification.

[This section completed on 5th September, forty-seventh day of imprisonment]

(d) *The Life of our Sanctification,* vs 8-10

This first section, vs. 1. to 10, the purpose of which is to explain the conception of sanctification, concludes in vs. 8-10 with the life of our sanctification. The sanctified life in its duality, vitality, finality and spirituality, is here explained.

(1) *Its Duality*

"We shall also live with Him", v. 8.

The life of our sanctification is not marked with singularity, it does not have being on its own, but with duality, it is life shared with another. We live through Christ. We live in Christ. We live with Christ. It is His life in which we share. It is in Him, in which we share. It is in Him, in the highest possible sense, that we live and move and have our being. The Lord Jesus in His upper room discourse declared, "Yet a little while, and the world seeth Me no more; but ye see Me; because I live, ye shall live also" (John 14:19). This is life originating from and supplied by the Risen Lord. The life of the Head is shared by all the members of His mystical body.

The Scriptures tell us that Christ is our Life. In Colossians, we have two Scriptures which complement each other.

"For ye are dead, and your life is hid with Christ in God" (Col. 3:3).

The Secret of our Life is Christ

We possess a life which the world knows nothing of, for it knows not Him. This life was concealed, buried away, covered over with Christ in God. What life is this!

"When Christ, who is our life, shall appear, then shall ye also appear with Him in glory" (Col. 3:4).

The Supply of our Life is Christ

The secretive life of the believer has for its increasing supply Christ Himself. He is our Life. "He that hath the son hath life" (I John 5:12).

(2) *Its Vitality*

"Knowing that Christ being raised from the dead dieth no more; death hath no more dominion over Him", v. 9.

The vitality of this life is unique. There is no other life which conquered death in its own domain and therefore is certain to triumph in the believer's heart. Sin when it is finished bringeth forth death, but this life is the finish of death.

"I am come," our Lord Jesus Christ declared of His people, "that they might have life, and that they might have it more abundantly" (John 10:10). The word translated more abundantly means "above the common". Yes, this life is above the common both in its nature and measure.

(3) *Its Finality*

"For in that He died, He died unto sin once; but in that He liveth, He liveth unto God" v. 10.

This life has its finality in God. It is eternal life. Once and once only it was subjected to death for the destruction of death but now its whole eternity is unto God. Death, unable to destroy it, was itself destroyed. Of that life our Lord Jesus spoke in John 10:17, 18.

"No man taketh it from me," He declared "but I lay it down of Myself. I have power to lay it down, and I have power to take it again. This commandment have I received of My Father" (John 10: 17, 18).

(4) *Its Spirituality*

"We believe that we shall also live, v. 8.

The life of our sanctification is spiritual life. We believe the emphasis is on faith. We walk by faith not by sight (II Cor. 5:7). Yes, and we need life to walk and that life is spiritual not carnal; it is also by faith.

So we learn that we are emancipated by sanctification.

[This section completed on Tuesday, 6th September, forth-eighth day of imprisonment]

2.   CRUCIFIXION OF SELF - EXHORTED
"Likewise we reckon ye also yourselves to be dead indeed unto sin, but alive unto God through Jesus Christ our Lord. Let not therefore sin reign in your mortal body, that ye should obey it in the lusts thereof" (Rom. 6:11, 12).

These two verses, which form the link between the section of the chapter on sanctification and that on consecration, exhort us to a four-fold duty. We are called to:

(1) a reckoning
(2) a recognising

(3) a rejecting
(4) a resisting

A Reckoning on Crucifixion in Regard to Sin

"Likewise reckon ye also yourselves to be dead indeed unto sin", v. 11.

The Greek word translated "reckon" occurs quite frequently in the New Testament. It is not always translated by the word "reckon". A study of some of these other translations will help us to grasp its full force.

(1) *The Thought of Contemplation*

In Mark 11:31, it is translated "reason", "And they *reasoned* with themselves". Here we have the thought of contemplation. The priests, scribes and elders contemplated the question put to them by the Lord Jesus, "The baptism of John was it from heaven or of men?" They meditated upon its import and the effect of whatever answer they could give. In order to get something of the meaning of our text, we might, using this thought of contemplation, paraphrase it thus, "Likewise make this the subject of your continuing contemplation that you are dead indeed unto sin. Meditate upon the great fact of your death on the Cross with Jesus Christ and its import to you now in this world of sin".

(2) *The Thought of Conclusion*

In Romans 3:28 it is translated by "conclude", "Therefore we *conclude* that a man is justified by faith".

Here we have the thought of a finding, a summing up, a great conclusion. As we contemplate the cross, in its relation to our identification with Christ in His crucifixion, this great conclusion of our own death to sin masters our soul. It becomes the deciding factor in my living. We could paraphrase it thus, "Likewise, let us conclude when sin would come against us that we are dead to it through our crucifixion with Christ".

(3) *The Thought of Certainty*

In Hebrews 11:19 it is translated "accounting", "Accounting that God was able to raise Him up, even from the dead".

Here the thought is that certainty of Abraham's faith. He was certain that Isaac, the child of promise, would live and not die. He climbed the mountain of testing with certainty, staggering not. Likewise we also can be certain of the conclusion of our contemplation. The truth of our text is absolutely certain. Let there be no doubt about it, be certain that we are dead indeed unto sin.

These three thoughts will help us to understand what it really means to reckon ourselves dead indeed unto sin.

(b) *A Recognising of Emancipation from Sin*
"But alive unto God through Jesus Christ our Lord" v. 11.

The thought of resurrection life in Christ is the recurring theme of these verses. We are emancipated from sin through our quickening with Christ in resurrection.

In verse 4, we have reference to newness of life; in verse 5, we have our sharing in His resurrection; in verse 8, we have our living with Him; and in verse 10, we have His living unto God.

It will be seen by a careful look at these verses that resurrection life is not only the life which escapes from the tomb but it is the life which exalts to the throne. It is the life which set out Saviour at God's "own right hand in the heavenly places, far above all principality and power, and might, and dominion, and every name that is named, not only in this world, but also in that which is to come; and hath put all things under His feet, and gave Him to be the Head over all things to the church, which is His body, the fullness of Him that filleth all in all" (Eph. 1:20-23).

It is the life which "hath raised us up together, and made us sit together in heavenly places in Christ Jesus" (Eph. 2:6).

The full titles of Christ are used. Christ in His Lordship is the great Emancipator. The word translated "through" is the Greek preposition "In". Our living unto God is in Christ. It is our duty as well as our privilege continually to recognise our life in Him, and as a glorious consequence our emancipation from sin. By this life we shatter the bars of the tomb of sin.

[This section completed Wednesday, 8th September, forth-ninth day of imprisonment]

(c) *A Rejecting of the domination of Sin*
"Let not sin therefore reign in your mortal body", v. 12.

In verse 6, we have the dethronement of the old man, the sinful nature or sin the root as distinct from sin the fruit. Although dethroned, sin ever seeks to recapture its lost throne. It is always striving to reign. "The flesh lusteth against the spirit" (Gal. 5:17). It is a tyrannical usurper.

The place where sin seeks dominion is our body, called here our mortal body, lit. our dying body. The body is the avenue and vehicle of sin. In Eden's garden the temptation was directed to the body; to the body's appetite, "good for food" the lust of the flesh; to the body's eye, "pleasant to the eye", the lust of the eye; and to the body's pride, "a tree to be desired to make one wise", the pride of life (Cp. Gen. 3:6 with I John 2:16).

Upon our body, our dying body, are the very marks of sin's dominion and here sin strives unceasingly for the mastery. Because of the cross we have authority to reject sin's dominion and power and to defeat its usurping demands. It is, therefore, our duty to reject continually the dominion and demands of the usurper, sin. It is thus that we enter into the crucifixion of self and emancipation of soul.

(d) A Resisting of the aspirations to sin

"That ye should obey it in the lusts thereof", v. 12.

The word translated "lust" means "over desire", "desire run riot". Sin in its desire and aspirations would bring us again into a state of slavery. The desires of sin are not to be obeyed but rather resisted. They are not to be countenanced. By resisting, we refuse to contemplate the sin to which we are tempted. Contemplation of sin leads to conception of sin and conception of sin to the actual commission of sin. The conception of sin is, of course, a breaking of God's law just as much as the commission of sin. It is sin committed in the heart.

The first step to sin then is its contemplation. Our Lord Jesus warned, "I say unto you, That whosoever looketh (contemplation of sin) on a woman to lust after her (conception of sin) hath committed adultery with her already in his heart (commission of sin)" (Matt. 5:28). It is our duty by the power of the cross to enter into the crucifixion of self and so resist the aspirations of sin.

The great truth of verse 6, the old man crucified with Christ, can be experienced in our lives as we continually reckon on crucifixion in regard to sin, recognise our emancipation from sin, reject the domination of sin and resist the aspirations to sin. It is to this reckoning, recognising, rejecting and resisting we are exhorted.

3.　THE CONSECRATION OF OUR SERVICE, vs. 13-23

Verse 14, the key verse of the whole chapter, is found in this section. Now there are three great operative words which lead us to experience the emancipation spoken of in verse 14. The first, in the section on sanctification, vs. 1-10, is the word "know", vs. 3, 6, 9. We experience sanctification by knowing. "Ye shall know the truth." Sanctify them through Thy truth (John 8:32; 17:17).

The second, in the section on crucifixion, vs. 11 and 12, is the word "reckon". We experience the crucifixion of self by reckoning.

The third, in the last section on consecration, vs. 13-23, is the word "yield", vs. 13, 16, 19. We experience consecration by yielding.

(a) *The Charter of our Consecration*

"For sin shall not have dominion over you; for ye are not under the law, but under grace. What then? shall we sin, because we are not under the law, but under grace? God forbid", vs. 14, 15.

Here is the charter of our emancipation, sanctification and consecration. Three dominions are brought before us:

(1) *the Dominion of Sin*. "Sin shall not have dominion over you."

(2) *The Dominion of Law*. "Ye are not under the law."

(3) *The Dominion of Grace*. "But under grace."

Notice the negation of the first two mentioned dominions. Sin shall *not* have dominion over you - "sin's dominion is broken". "Ye are *not* under law", "the law's dominion broken". The reference here is to the law as a road *to* life, as a way of justification and not to the law as a rule *of* life, the way in which the justified walk. The place of the law in the believer's life is fully discussed by Paul in the next chapter as we shall see. We are under grace. Grace is the charter of our consecration. Every benefit of redemption, every boon of remission and every blessing of reconciliation is ours by grace alone. As subjects of the dominion or throne of grace we can enter into all the blessings of entire consecration to God. This is our right and privilege.

(b) *The Commencement of our Consecration*

"But God be thanked, that ye were the servants of sin, but ye have obeyed from the heart that form of doctrine which was delivered you. Being then made free from sin, ye became the servants of righteousness", vs. 17, 18.

This verse sets forth the spiritual experience which marks the commencement of our consecration.

There are six great facts here declared.

(1) *What We Were*

"Ye were the servants of sin", v. 17.

The word "servant" is literally bond-servant or slave. Paul had in mind the Roman slave.

Slaves were in *bondage*. They had no freedom. Their liberty was taken from them. They were bound by their master. His will was their will and he commanded their every action.

We were in bondage, the bondage of sin. We had no freedom. Our liberty was taken from us. We were bound by our master, sin. It ruled and dominated our lives by the corruption of our natures and the tyranny of our debasing habits.

Thomas Goodwin, the Puritan, said, that before entering the pulpit when his heart was not humble as it ought to be, he took a walk up and down among his former sins. This always brought humiliation to his heart and stirred gratitude in his soul to God.

John Newton, the famous preacher and more famous hymn writer, once the slave driver and blasphemous seaman, had the text Deuteronomy 15:15 printed in large capitals and hung over his study desk. "And Thou Shalt Remember That Thou Wast a Bondman in The Land of Egypt, And The Lord Thy God Redeemed Thee."

Slaves were burdened. They had to bear the burden and heat of the day of toil. Like Joseph in prison they were laid in iron, Psalm 105:18.

We were burdened. The load of sin was upon our back and like Bunyan's pilgrim we could not ease ourselves from its heartbreaking weight.

Slaves were beaten. The taskmaster's whip often lashed the naked bodies of the slaves. Punishment, cruel and unrelenting, was oftentimes their lot; blood, sweat and tears their daily portion. We were beaten. Our sins were not only found out by others but they found us out. The backlash of our sinning struck us again and again. The scourge of a troubled conscience, mightily awakened at times, whipped our guilty and depressed souls.

We must never forget what we were, slaves in the slave market of sin. Isaiah's exhortation, "Look unto the rock whence ye are hewn, and the hole of the pit whence ye are digged" (Isa. 51:1) we need continually to obey.

(2) *What We Heard*

"That form of doctrine which was delivered unto you", v. 17.

This word translated "form" merits attention. It literally means "impress". It is translated "pattern" in Hebrews 8:5, "As Moses was admonished of God when he was about to make the tabernacle; for, see, saith He, that thou make all things according to the *pattern* shewed to thee in the Mount". The thought here is exactness. Moses dare not change the Divine plan by taking from or adding to. It is also translated "print".

"Except I shall see in His hands the *print* of the nails" (John 20: 25).

Here again the thought is exactness. Thomas wanted to see the exact mark or imprint which the nails made in the hands and feet of the Lord Jesus. That mark, part of the finished work, is unchangeable. It remains exactly the same.

The form, the pattern of doctrine is Divine like the tabernacle and nothing must be added to it or taken from it.

The form, the print of doctrine is finished like the wounds of our Lord Jesus Christ. It is a finished work which we declare.

It is by the delivery of Divinely finished doctrine that we are saved. This is what we heard, the exact, the Divinely finished counsel of God. By no other message are the slaves of sin redeemed. The word "delivered" Paul uses in I Corinthians 15:3. "For I delivered unto you first of all that which I also received." It means "to give over to" and is used of the deliverance of the prisoner to the judge for judgment. "Lest at any time the adversary *deliver* thee to the judge, and the judge *deliver* thee to the officer, and thou be cast into prison" (Matt. 5:25).

The preacher's work is to give over to the sinner the truth of God, in such a manner that the sinner can no more escape from giving the verdict than the judge can when the lawful prisoner is before him for judgment.

(3) *What We did*

"Obeyed from the heart", v. 17.

The Greek preposition translated here by "from" is literally "out of". We obey out of the heart, not out of the head. Salvation is a heart work not a head work. "Believe in thine heart " for with the heart man believeth" (Rom. 10:9, 10). The word "obey" means "to hearken submissively unto". It has the thought of submission to irresistible authority. It is used of the obedience of the winds and waves (Matt 8:27) of the unclean spirits (Mark 1:27) and of the tree (Luke 17:6). This is the effectual call of the gospel as distinguished from the common call.

(4) *What We Experienced*

"Being then made free from sin", v. 18.

Blessed Emancipation! Glorious Freedom!

With Charles Wesley we sing:

Long my imprisoned spirit lay,
Fast bound in sin and nature's night:

Thine eyes diffused a quickening ray,
I woke, the dungeon flamed with light;
My chains fell off, my heart was free,
I rose, went forth and followed Thee.

We are free from sin's penalty; that is our justification.

We are free from sin's power; that is our emancipation.

We are free from sin's pollution; that is our sanctification.

We shall be free from sin's presence; that is our glorification.

(5) *What We Are*

"Ye became the servants of righteousness", v. 18.

We have exchanged masters. We are now the slaves of Christ. His service is perfect freedom. His yoke is easy and His burden is light. Righteousness, not sin, rules us and that is without punishment; for righteousness is the fruit of "love, joy, peace, longsuffering, gentleness, goodness, faith, meekness and temperance" and, says the Book, "against such there is no law" (Gal. 5: 22, 23). What a contrast. Slaves of sin now slaves of righteousness.

(6) *What We Are To Do*

"But God be thanked", v. 17.

We are to bless God with hearts filled with thankfulness and praise. Consecration commenced in this way shall continue and be consummated.

O thou my soul, bless God the Lord;
and all that in me is
Be stirred up His holy name
to magnify and bless.
Bless, O my soul, the Lord thy God,
and not forgetful be
Of all His gracious benefits
He hath bestow'd on thee.
(Psalm 103:1, 2).
What shall I render to the Lord
for all His gifts to me?
I'll of salvation take the cup,
On God's name will I call'
I'll pay my vows now to the Lord
before his people all.

~ (Psalm 116:12-14).

[This section completed on the fifty-first day of imprisonment: Friday, 9th September]

(c) *The Characters of our Consecration*

"Neither yield ye your members as instruments of unrighteousness unto sin; but yield yourselves unto God, as those that are alive from the dead, and your members as instruments of righteousness unto God", v. 13. "Know ye not, that to whom ye yield yourselves servants to obey, his servants ye are to whom ye obey; whether of sin unto death, or of obedience unto righteousness?" v. 16.

"I speak after the manner of men because of the infirmity of your flesh; for as ye have yielded your members servants to uncleanness and to iniquity unto iniquity; even so now yield your members servants to righteousness unto holiness", v. 19.

Paul draws a parallel here between our service in sin and our service to God. The secret of both is found in the word "yield". The word literally means "to set along side of", "to present". It is translated "present" in Romans 12:1. "Ye *present* your bodies a living sacrifice".

It is also used of Christ presenting the church in glory to Himself. "That he might present it (the church) to Himself a glorious church, not having spot, or wrinkle, or any such thing; but that it should be holy and without blemish" (Eph 5: 27). The word has in it the thought of handing over, surrender.

(1) *Yielding Dedicates the Whole Man*

"Yield yourselves unto God", v. 13.

This entails the dedication of the whole man. Everything the man is, everything the man has, everything the man does is included in and influenced by his yielding. This is absolute unconditional, full surrender to God.

In our servitude to sin, the world, the flesh and the devil were in full control.

In Ephesians 2:2, 3 our former estate is described thus:

"Wherein in time past ye walked according to the course of this world, according to the prince of the power of the air, the spirit that now worketh in the children of disobedience: Among whom also we all had our conversation in times past in the lusts of our flesh, fulfilling the desires of the flesh and of the mind; and were by nature the children of wrath, even as others."

Notice:

1. *Our Course was the World*
    "Ye walked according to the course of this world", v. 2.
2. *Our Control was the Devil*
    "According to the prince of the power of the air", v. 2.
3. *Our Conversation was the Flesh*
    "We all had our conversation (manner of life) in the lusts of the flesh", v. 3.
    Now Christ should be our all in all.
1. *Christ our Course*
    "I am the way".
2. *Christ our Control*
    "The truth".
3. *Christ our Conversation*
    "The Life (John 14:6).
    Yielding to Christ dedicates the whole man.

(2) *Yielding Demands Every Member*
    "Yield ye your members as instruments of righteousness unto God", v. 13.
    "Yield your members servants to righteousness unto holiness", v. 19.
    The word translated "instrument" here is translated "armour" in Romans 13:12 and "weapons" in II Corinthians 10:4. The armour, the weapons, the instrument, are useless except put to their proper use by someone with power. Our members must be wielded by the power of God. Here we have God's sovereignty in our consecration. We are passive instruments for His service. In verse 19 our yielded members are called "servants to righteousness". The servant has life, will and intelligence which he exercises on behalf of his master. There is a great difference between the inanimate instrument and the living servant. In the servant we have the truth of personal responsibility in our consecration. We are active servants in His service.

(3) *Yielding Declares the Master*
    "To whom ye yield yourselves servants to obey, his servants ye are", v. 16.
    It is not difficult to see whose servants we are. Our obedience demonstrates this in an unconcealable manner. Righteousness and holiness are evidences which cannot be gainsaid that our master is the Lord Christ. No matter what we profess, uncleanness and iniquity declare that our master is sin.

(d) *The Consummation of our Consecration*

"For when ye were the servants of sin, ye were free from righteousness. What fruit had ye then in those things whereof ye are now ashamed? for the end of those things is death. But now being made free from sin, and become servants to God, ye have your fruit unto holiness, and the end everlasting life", vs. 20-22.

In these verses, we have the consummation of our consecration in right-eousness contrasted with the consummation of our degradation in sin. The contrast is three-fold, it is a contrast of freedoms, fruits and finishes.

(1) *Two Freedoms*

(a) "When ye were the servants of sin, ye were *free* from righteousness", v. 20. Freedom from righteousness.

(b) "But now being made *free* from sin, and become servants to God", v. 22. Freedom from sin. The consummation of our degradation is freedom from righteousness. The consummation of our consecration is freedom from sin. What a contrast!

(2) *Two Fruits*

(a) "What *fruit* had you then in those things whereof ye are now ashamed?", v. 21. This test is in the form of a question. We who lived in sin know only too well the dark answer. How horrible is the fruit of sin!

(b) "Ye have your *fruit* unto holiness", v. 2. The consummation of our degradation is the nameless fruit of darkness.

The consummation of our consecration is the numerous fruit of holiness. What a contrast!

(3) *Two finishes*

(a) "The *end* of those things is death", v. 21.

(b) "and the *end* everlasting life", v. 22.

The consummation of our degradation in sin is the woeful finish of ever-lasting death.

The consummation of our consecration in righteousness is the wonderful finish of everlasting life. What a contrast!

(e) *The Conclusion of the Whole Matter*

"For the wages of sin is death; but the gift of God is eternal life through Jesus Christ our Lord", v. 23.

This verse is the grand conclusion of the whole epistle so far.

We have seen *man rebelling and ruined in* chapters 1, 2 and 3. "For the wages of sin is death."

We have seen *man redeemed and reconciled* in chapters 4 and 5, that is "the gift of God".

We have seen *man raised and restored* in chapter six, that is "eternal life".

Yes, and

It is all, write it in golden words, "Through Jesus Christ our Lord".

[This section completed on Monday, 12th September, fifty-fourth day of imprisonment]

7 The law
of God

IN THIS CHAPTER Paul deals with a most important subject, the law of God. The law of God (that is, the moral law of God which is eternal, in distinction from the ceremonial law of God which was temporal and typical, has a most important function in the economy of grace and is not abrogated or abolished as far as the believer is concerned. How different is this language of the apostle, "I delight in the law of God after the inward man" and the frivolous attitude of those who deny the authority of the law of God in this day of grace. Paul here hits hard, by the inspiration of the Holy Ghost, at the pernicious doctrine of the antinomians, - those who deny the obligations of the moral law.

When we read "we are not under the law but under grace" we must understand in what sense "the law" is here used. This undoubtedly has to do with our salvation. The law as the road to life, the path of justification, because of the weakness of the flesh, in unavailing. I cannot be justified by the law. Christ, who is grace incarnate, as the road to life, the way of justification, is all-availing. I am justified freely by His grace.

In this sense I am not under the law but under grace. The law of God is my rule of life, however, because I am under the law of Christ. It is His yoke and through grace it is an easy yoke and a light burden. Therefore, I delight in it after the inward man.

It is concerning this important place of the law in the economy of grace that Paul speaks when he says "being not without law to God, but under the law to Christ" (I Cor. 9:21).

In this chapter, we have many important aspects of the law of God both in its failure through the weakness of the flesh to be the road to life and in its spirituality and obligatory character to the new man in Christ.

1.   THE LIMITATION OF THE LAW, vs. 1-6

In these verses we have set forth the extent of the jurisdiction of the law, where its dominion ceases and how its obligations are no longer valid.

The reference here is to the law as the way of life, the rule of justification saying to us, "Do these things and thou shalt live" (Gal. 3:12).

These verses expound the two covenants revealing the two marriages as in the life of the patriarch Abraham. Read Galatians 4: 22-31.

(a) *The First Marriage - The Covenant of Works*
"Know ye not, brethren (for I speak to them that know the law) how that the law hath dominion over a man as long as he liveth?"

"For the woman which hath an husband is bound by the law to her husband so long as he liveth; but if the husband be dead she is loosed from the law of her husband. So then if, while her husband liveth, she be married to another man, she shall be called an adulteress: but if her husband be dead, she is free from that law; so that she is no adulteress, though she be married to another man", vs. 1-3.

The dominion of the law, the bond of this marriage, ceases at death. The woman is loosed when her husband dies. While he lives she dare not take another man for that would be adultery. When he dies, however, the law has no more dominion, the marriage contract is dissolved, and she is absolutely emancipated from its claims and obligations.

(b) *The Second Marriage - The Covenant of Grace*
"Wherefore, my brethren, ye also are become dead to the law by the body of Christ; that ye should be *married* to another, even to him who is raised from the dead" v. 4. The dominion of the law as a covenant of works, as far as we are concerned, has ceased. Death has put an end to its jurisdiction. The marriage tie is dissolved, for we "are become dead to the law by the body of Christ". It was through that body that God condemned sin in the flesh (Rom. 8:3).

It was through that body on the Cross that Christ dissolved our marriage contract with the law in the covenant of works. "Blotting out the handwriting of ordinances that was against us, which was contrary to us, and took it out of the way, nailing it to his Cross" (Col. 2:14).

It was through that body we became dead to the law. We are now legally married to another even to the Risen Christ.

(c) *The Fruit of the First Marriage*

"For when we were in the flesh, the motions of sins, which were by the law, did work in our members to bring forth *fruit* unto death", v. 5. The fruit of the first marriage was death. Four words are important, "flesh", "sins", "law" and "death".

The flesh is the old nature, the old Adam in us; being in the flesh is being in Adam. Sins are the fruit of this old root.

The law, here meaning the road to life. By it we are condemned. We are not able to attain to its standards and its sentence is passed upon us.

Death, the sentence of the law. Having failed to live by the law, we are condemned to die by the law. This is the fruit of our first marriage by the covenant of works.

(d) *The Fruit of the Second Marriage*

"That we should bring forth *fruit* unto God", v. 4.

"But now we are delivered from the law, that being dead wherein we were held; that we should serve in newness of spirit, and not in the oldness of the letter", v. 6.

From the law as the way of justification we are delivered. "But now we are delivered from the law." Its sentence of death cannot be passed on to us. The power of the flesh (the root) and the sins (the fruit) are also broken.

"Being dead wherein we were held." Death has smashed their dominion.

We serve our new husband not in the oldness of the letter which was the service of Hagar and gendereth to bondage, Galatians 4:24, but in the newness of spirit which gendereth to life and freedom.

This is the fruit of the second marriage by the covenant of grace.

2.   THE OPERATION BY THE LAW, vs. 7-14

This section sets forth the operation of the law in the realm of sin. The nature of the law and its workings are here lucidly expounded in all too brief verses.

(a) *The Revelation of Spirituality in the Law*

"Wherefore the law is holy, and the commandment holy, and just, and good", v. 12.

"For we know that the law is spiritual; but I am carnal, sold under sin", v. 14.

There is nothing wrong with the law, not a precept too many or a promise too few, if a man use it lawfully. "Knowing this, that the law is not made for righteous man, but for the lawless and disobedient, for the ungodly and for sinners, for unholy and profane, for murderers of fathers and murderers of mothers, for manslayers, for whoremongers, for them that defile themselves with mankind, for menstealers, for liars, for perjured persons, and if there be any other thing that is contrary to sound doctrine" (I Tim. 1:9, 10).

The law, being the revelation of the will of God, is stamped with the attributes of God himself. In its nature it is like its Divine Author, the Lawgiver of the Universe.

It is spiritual. God is a spirit (John 4:24). The law is spiritual as opposed to fleshly, divine as opposed to human, and heavenly as opposed to carnal.

It is holy. God is holy. He is addressed as Holy Father (John 17:11). The word translated "holy" means separate, set apart for divine use. The law of God is like no other law. It is separate, kept apart for divine service.

It is just. God is just (Rom. 3:26). The word translated "holy" means righteous. The law of God is righteous., There is nothing unfair about its precepts or punishments. Justice marks its whole character.

It is good. God is good (Mark 10:18). The law is good in itself and does good to those who are obedient to its commandments. In the revelation of the law we see the spirituality, holiness, righteousness and goodness of God manifested. The law, then, is not to be despised but rather honoured and obeyed.

As the way of life, the road of justification, it is weak, not of itself, but because of the weakness of the flesh. It is spiritual but I am carnal, sold under sin. Because of this, it cannot justify the sinner nor give him life. "For if there had been a law given which could have given life, verily righteousness should have been by the law. But the scripture hath concluded all under sin, that the promise by faith of Jesus Christ might be given to them that believe" (Gal. 3:21-23).

(b) *The Realisation of Sin Through the Law*, vs. 7-13

The law, being spiritual and holy, just and good, cannot however, bring us to a life-giving knowledge of God yet it can bring us to a legal knowledge of Him.

Through the law the commands of God are known and hence the knowledge of what is right and what is wrong. Therefore by the law is the knowledge of sin (Rom. 3:2).

(1) *The Realisation of What Sin Is.*

"What shall we say then? Is the law sin? God forbid. Nay, I had not known sin, but by the law; for I had not known lust, except the law had said, Thou shalt not covet", v. 7.

Paul again is most careful to vindicate the integrity of the law. He asks the question, "Is the law sin?" and then follows that frequent exclamation translated in our New Testament by "God forbid", but meaning literally, "May it not be!" It is a very strong exclamation of complete negation of the question. It occurs ten times in the epistle; besides this verse it is found in chapter 3:4, 6, 31; chapter 6:2, 15; chapter 7:13; chapter 9:14; chapter 11:1, 11.

The law is not sin, but by the law sin is known. The commandment reveals God's will and its violation is sin. Paul illustrates this by quoting the tenth commandment. It is significant that Paul chooses this the last of the commandments. The reason is that at the heart of the violation of any of the other nine is the sin of covetousness. Go down each of the two tables of the law and it will be easily seen that covetousness will lead to the breaking of all the commandments.

Covetousness begets idolatry which violates the third commandment.

Covetousness begets blasphemy which violates the third commandment.

Covetousness begets Sabbath desecration which violates the fourth commandment.

Covetousness begets rebellion which violates the fifth commandment.

Covetousness begets hate which violated the sixth commandment.

Covetousness begets fleshly lust which violates the seventh commandment.

Covetousness begets robbery which violates the eighth commandment.

Covetousness begets falsehood which violates the ninth commandment.

Covetousness itself violates the tenth commandment.

As love is the fulfilling of the whole law so lust is the violation of the whole law.

So Paul used the commandment the breaking of which lies at the heart of every sin. Sin is realised for what it is through the law. The apostle argues thus. "I had not known lust except the law had said, Thou shalt not covet."

(2) The Realisation of What Sin Does, vs. 8-11.

There are six aspects of sin in these verses.

1. *Sin Sleeping*

"For without the law sin was dead. For I was alive without the law once", vs. 8, 9.

In chapter 5 we read until the law sin was in the world; but sin is not imputed when there is no law" (Rom. 6:13). "I was alive without the law once," says Paul. He is not of course speaking about being alive unto God. Law or no law he was in a state of death. He is rather speaking about his state before he realised by a knowledge of the law what sin is and what it does. In this state the words of chapter 5 could be applied to his experience. Then although he was alive like Nabal of old when the King's word reached him "his heart died within him, and he became as a stone" (I Sam. 25:37).

2. *Sin Reviving*

"But when the commandment came, sin revived, and I died", v. 9.

When the law of God became known and its claims were brought home to the conscience by the conviction of its holy truth, sin no longer slept but revived. Its presence and power were soon discovered in the life. The more the law thundered loudly in our ears the more we felt the power of sin chaining our life. Sinai spelt subjection to our whole being because of sin.

3. *Sin Working*

"But sin, taking occasion by the commandment, wrought in me all manner of concupiscence", v. 8.

Sin is a worker and is revived through the soul's knowledge of the law, it works unceasingly for the accomplishment of its end, even the eternal death of the sinner. Sin takes impulse by the law because of the weakness of the flesh and works out in the heart all manner of lust. The word translated "concupiscence" is the same word translated "lust" in verse 7. All manner of lust refers to the violation of the whole law for lust as we have already seen lies at the heart of such a violation. O the damnable workings of sin!

The Lord Jesus surveyed them and exclaimed, "For out of the heart proceed evil thoughts, murders, adulteries, fornications, thefts, false witness, blasphemies" (Matt. 15:19).

Thank God, Christ was manifested to take away our sins and to destroy the works of the devil (I John 3:5, 8). Hallelujah!

4. *Sin Deceiving*

"For sin, taking occasion by the commandment, deceived me", v. 11.

The age-long tactics of sin lie uncovered. Sin entered into the world along the avenue of deception. The crafty serpent deceived the woman, taking occasion by the commandment and the law was violated and sin triumphed. How many times have these stages been repeated in our own experience? How terrible are the deceptions of sin! How subtly sin takes impulse or occasion by the commandment!

5. *Sin Slaying*

"And the commandment, which was ordained to life, I found to be unto death. For sin, taking occasion by the commandment, deceived me, and by it slew me", vs. 10, 11. "Sin, when it is finished, bringeth forth death," James 1:15. Sin slays. It leaves the slaughtered millions of humanity in its wake. How fearful is its execution! Its instruments of slaughter we have all experienced. It first seduces and then it slays. Sin's deceptions lead to the soul's death.

6. *Sin Exceeding*

"Was then that which is good made death unto me? God forbid. But sin, that it might appear sin, working death in me by that which is good; that sin by the commandment might become exceeding sinful" (Rom, 7:13).

Paul finishes this section as he commenced it by vindicating the integrity of the law (see v. 7). "Was then that which is good (i.e. the law, see previous verse) made death unto me?" he asks. "May it not be!" he exclaims. Rather the law is the great X-ray revealing sin working death in me so that sin by the revelation of the law is seen to be exceeding sinful. By the operation of the law its spirituality is revealed to the sinner and then the realisation of what sin is and what it does, is brought home to the sinner's heart.

3.   THE CONFRONTATIONS THROUGH THE LAW, vs. 15-20

"For that which I do I allow not; for what I would, that do I not; but what I hate, that do I. If then I do that which I would not, I consent unto the law that it is good. Now then it is no more I that do it, but sin that dwelleth in me. For I know that in me (that is, in my flesh,) dwelleth no good thing; for to will is present with me; but how to perform that which is good I find not. For the good that I would I do not; but the evil which I would not, that I

do. Now if I do that I would not, it is no more I that do it, but sin that dwelleth in me", vs. 15-20.

The recognition of the law as spiritual and acceptance of its divine decrees leads to the confrontation of flesh and spirit, the old and new natures, in the believer. "For the flesh lusteth against the Spirit, and the Spirit against the flesh; and these are contrary the one to the other; so that ye cannot do the things ye would" (Gal. 5:17).

This confrontation arising from a recognition and acceptance of the goodness of God's law is told by Paul here in all its grim reality. His attitude is right but his actions are wrong. The law is not understood in its relationship to Christ nor is sin seen in its rightful place on the cross, hence the actions which do not tally with the attitude. He consents to the law as being good, v. 16, but sin dwelling in him leads to its transgression. He learns again the total depravity of the old man and confesses "I know that in me (that is, in my flesh,) dwelleth no good thing", v. 18. He is caught up in bitter conflict and cries out "For that which I do I allow not; for what I would, that do I not; but what I hate, that do I", v. 15.

"For the good that I would I do not; but the evil which I would not, that I do. Now if I do that I would not, it is no more I that do it, but sin that dwelleth in me", vs. 19, 20. He is faced with a great problem, the problem of how to perform that which is good, v. 18. This problem is solved in the remaining verses of the chapter (which are really the beginning of chapter 8 and should be read as such) and in chapter 8 itself.

4.   **THE EMANCIPATION FROM THE LAW, vs. 21-25**
      "I find then a law, that, when I would do good, evil is present with me. For I delight in the law of God after the inward man; but I see another law in my members, warring against the law of my mind, and bringing me into captivity to the law of sin which is in my members. O wretched man that I am! who shall deliver me from the body of this death? I thank God through Jesus Christ our Lord. So then with the mind I myself serve the law of God; but with the flesh the law of sin", vs. 21-25.

When emancipation from the law is spoken of, the reference, of course, is to the bondage, guilt, and death, resulting from the knowledge and operation of the law in our hearts. We are emancipated through Christ from the law as the path of justification, the way to life. We are not emancipated from its moral precepts nor do we as believers desire any such liberty. We gladly serve, as Paul says, with "the mind", v. 25 (that is the renewed mind which is the same as the inward man of v. 22) the law of God.

The three laws of v. 23 are to be carefully distinguished. Paul says, "I see *another law* in my members, warring against *the law of my mind*, and bringing me into captivity to *the law of sin* which is in my members."

1. Another law.
2. The law of my mind.
3. The law of sin.

The law of his mind is (as can be clearly seen in verse 25 "with the mind I myself serve the law of God") the law of God. It is the law of God not as the way of salvation but the way in which the saved delight to walk, see v. 22. It is in reality the law of Christ for as believers we are "not without law to God, but under the law to Christ" (I Cor. 9:21).

The law in Paul's members which wars against the law of Christ is of course the law of the old nature. It is the sceptre of the old Adam outstretched in rebellion in the heart. When this law triumphs over the law of Christ the soul is brought into captivity or bondage to the law of sin. The law of sin is the law by which we have the knowledge of sin. It is the law of God as the way of justification which was ordained to life but found rather to be unto death, v. 10. Verses two and three of the next chapter make this clear.

Now the law which wars against the law of Christ in Paul's members he called "the body of this death", v. 23. There was a torture well known to the Romans to whom Paul is writing and no doubt he has the same in mind when he uses this phrase.

A dead body was fastened to the body of the sentenced prisoner. It was strapped on forehead to forehead, nose to nose, lips to lips, chest to chest, arms to arms, hands to hands, loins to loins, legs to legs and feet to feet. In fact the living man became a human cross on which the corpse hung. Everywhere the prisoner moved he was forced to carry the body of this death. The power of death, of course, slowly but surely overcame life and soon there were two corpses instead of one.

Paul calls the old nature in him "the body of this death", and cries out "O wretched man that I am! who shall deliver me?"

Thank God there is deliverance, for the cry has no sooner left his lips till he bursts forth in the doxology, "I thank God through Jesus Christ".

The next chapter expounds the way of this deliverance from the bondage, guilt and curse of the law to which "the body of this death" subjects us.

*[**This chapter completed on Thursday, 15th September, 1966:**
fifty-seventh day of imprisonment]*

8 The chapter of
the Spirit

IN ORDER TO get the real force of this chapter we should read from verse twenty-one of the previous chapter. The last section of chapter seven is really the beginning of that section of the epistle contained in chapter eight. There were no chapter divisions in the original scriptures and sometimes these are of such an artificial nature that in heeding them the full force of a passage is missed. Without a doubt this is the chapter of the Spirit of God. Altogether in the whole epistle there are twenty-six references to the Spirit of God in his various titles. Eight of these occur outside this eighth chapter, in chapters 1:4, 5:5, 9:1, 14:17, 15:13, 16, 19, 30. The other eighteen occur in this chapter so we have good reason to call it the chapter of the Spirit.

These 18 references are found in (1) v. 1, (2) v. 2, (3) v. 4, (4) v. 5, (5) v. 9, (6) v. 9. (7) v. 9, (8) v. 10, (9) v. 11, (10) v. 11, (11) v. 13, (12) c. 14, (13) v. 15, (14) v. 16, (15) v. 23, (16) v. 26, (17) v. 26, (18) v. 27. Someone has rightly called the Holy Spirit the Executor of the Godhead and in this chapter we have His work expounded as the executor of the New Covenant sealed in all its covenant blessings of justification and sanctification by the precious blood of Christ.

An executor makes good the provisions of the will to the beneficiaries. In this chapter all the provisions of the New Covenant, as set forth in the previous chapters, are made good to the believers, the beneficiaries under this New Covenant of grace, by the Spirit of God.

There are ten great truths set forth here concerning pneumatology, the doctrine of the Holy Spirit.

Needless to say the Deity and Personality of the Spirit are presupposed and attested throughout the whole chapter.

1.   **THE LAW OF THE SPIRIT**
"There is therefore now no condemnation to them which are in Christ Jesus, who walk not after the flesh, but after the Spirit. For the law of the spirit of life in Christ Jesus hath made me free from the law of sin and death", vs. 1, 2.

Herein are five great characteristics of the Spirit's law.

(a) *The Designation of the Law*
"The law of the Spirit of life", v. 2.

The Spirit's law stands out in sharp contrast to the law of sin and death mentioned in the same verse. The law and its sad consequences we have pondered in chapter seven. It was ordained to life but bound to be unto death, chapter 7: 10.

The law of the Spirit is designed "of life" because it brings life, eternal life, to the soul. Where the other law failed, this law triumphed. Where the other law stands impotent, this law stands omnipotent. The life of the Spirit is life in every realm and where this law rules, sin must yield its sceptre and death its throne. It is this law of life that we, the children of death, require for the salvation of our souls.

(b) *The Domain of the Law*
"In Christ Jesus", v. 1, 2,

The domain of this law is described as "in Christ Jesus". In Adam the law of sin and death had its domain. Under the federal Headship of Adam that law wielded its sceptre and we bowed in subjection to its sway.

We are no longer in Adam. We have a new federal head even Christ, the Second Man, the Lord from heaven. Once we were without Christ, "being aliens from the commonwealth of Israel, and strangers from the covenants of promise, having no hope, and without God in the world (Eph. 2:12). Now we are in Christ and are no longer afar off but are made nigh by the blood of Christ" (Eph. 2:13).

Outside of Christ is not the domain of the Holy Spirit or His law. In Christ the law of the Spirit rules supreme and we are happy subjects of its precepts.

(c) *The Deliverance of the Law*

"Hath made me free from the law of sin and death", v. 2.

In the final verses of chapter seven, Paul groans in his captivity and cries out, "Who shall deliver me from the body of this death?" (Rom. 7:24). The body of this death dominates and tyrannises over him because he is subject to the law of sin and death. The law of God has brought home to him the knowledge of his sin and pronounced upon him the great sentence of death. The old nature has made him chained in his actions and controls the members of his body.

When the Spirit comes, the curse of the law is removed and its hideous tyranny broken and he is freed from the law of sin and death.

The mighty King of Kings, with healing in His wings,

To every captive soul a full deliverance brings;

And through the vacant cells the song of triumph rings;

The Holy Ghost has come!

(d) *The Demonstration of the Law*

"Who walk not after the flesh, but after the Spirit", v. 1.

The law of the Spirit of life in all its power is demonstrated in the walk of the believer. The word translated "after" is literally "according to". We no longer walk according to the lusts of the flesh, the pleasures of the flesh and the sins of the flesh, but we walk now by the law of the Spirit of life, according to the desires, pleasures and holiness of the Spirit. The Spirit's law of life is demonstrated in the living of the believer. Our faith justifies us before God but our works justify us before men. "For faith without works is dead" (Jas. 2:26). Faith, true faith, is not a dead faith, but a living faith producing fruit unto holiness and the end everlasting life (Rom. 6:22).

(e) *The Declaration of the Law*

"There is therefore now no condemnation to them that are in Christ Jesus", v. 1.

The declaration of the law of God as the way of justification, is condemnation on me the sinner. I cannot keep its precepts and its curse falls upon me. I stand condemned and my heart echoes the dread sentence of the law. I know condemnation, of heart, of conscience, of mind and of soul. But now in Christ

Jesus I stand justified. I hear the sweet declaration of the law of the Spirit of life, "There is therefore now no condemnation". This grand conclusion rests upon the whole foundation of the great truths of chapters four, five, six and seven. The law of the Spirit, on the basis of the mighty reconciling, redeeming, raising and restoring work of Christ in death and resurrection, declares I can never be condemned. Hallelujah! Ten thousand times Hallelujah![1]

The sweet irreversible and irrevocable message echoes in my heart, my conscience, my mind and my soul., It depends not on what I am but upon what Christ is. Christ is not the great I was, Christ is the great I am. It depends not on what I do but upon what Christ has done. This immutable decree of the law of the Spirit of life has illuminated and emancipated my whole being.

> *No condemnation now I dread;*
> *Jesus, and all in Him is mine!*
> *Alive in Him, my living Head,*
> *And clothed in righteousness Divine,*
> *Bold I approach the eternal Throne,*
> *And claim the crown, through Christ my own.*

**[This section completed on Saturday, 17th September, 1966,
fifty-ninth day of imprisonment]**

2.   THE WALK OF THE SPIRIT
"For what the law could not do, in that it was weak through the flesh, God sending his own Son in the likeness of sinful flesh, and for sin, condemned sin in the flesh; that the righteousness of the law might be fulfilled in us, who walk not after the flesh, but after the Spirit", vs. 3-4.

The walk of the Spirit is the King's Highway as described in Isaiah 35:8-10: "And an highway shall be there, and a way, and it shall be called, The way of holiness; the unclean shall not pass over it; but it shall be for those: the wayfaring men, though fools, shall not err therein. No lion shall be there, nor any ravenous beast shall go up thereon, it shall not be found there; but the redeemed shall walk there. And the ransomed of the Lord shall return, and come to Zion with songs and everlasting joy upon their heads; they shall obtain joy and gladness, and sorrow and sighing shall flee away."

(a) *The Walk obstructed by the Law*

"For what the law could not do, in that it was weak through the flesh", v. 3.

The law decreed that, "the man that doeth them (i.e. the commandments) shall live in them" (Gal. 3:12). Because of the weakness of the flesh man could not do the commandments of the law so the law obstructed the King's Highway. What was intended for a door became instead an insurmountable barrier, for man, through sin, had lost the key with which the door could be opened.

The unclean cannot walk this way and man, unclean by the leprosy of sin, was therefore legally prohibited. The law which was ordained to life is actually found to be the obstacle to that very life it was ordained to bestow (Rom. 7:10). Thus the walk of the Spirit was obstructed by the Law.

(b) *The Walk opened by the Son*

"God sending His own Son in the likeness of sinful flesh, and for sin, condemned sin in the flesh", v. 3. The Son of God incarnate (Christ in the likeness of sinful flesh, and mark, not sinful flesh but in the likeness of sinful flesh) has by the obedience of His impeccable life and the shedding of His incorruptible blood opened the King's Highway for His people. He has provided the key and opened the door. The law is no obstacle to Him, for He fulfilled every jot and tittle of its requirements. He magnified the law and made it honourable. Notice the four views of the Son in the verse.

(1) The Sent One - "God sent His own Son".

(2) The Seen One - "in the likeness of sinful flesh".

(3) The Substitute One - "for sin".

(4) The Sinless One - "condemned sin in the flesh".

(c) *The Walk occupied by the Saint*

"That the righteousness of the law might be fulfilled in us, who walk not after the flesh", v. 4. The unclean cannot occupy the King's Highway. Uncleanness is a characteristic of the flesh. We who are not in the flesh can therefore occupy this way. Isaiah talks of the redeemed and ransomed walking in this way. The righteousness of the law which Christ has fulfilled and which by justification has been imputed to us, marks us as both ransomed and redeemed and fits us to walk this way of holiness. The word translated "righteousness" is literally "requirement". The requirement of the law is more than met for us by the Lord Jesus and we have the right to all the covenant privileges, one of which is access to and enjoyment of this glorious way. The way is occupied by the saint.

(d) *The Walk ordered by the Spirit*

"But after the Spirit", v. 4.

The Spirit of God orders the walk. He is in complete control. He leads and guides. He marks out the path and points the way. It is a walk by faith and not by sight. He leads through valleys and over mountains. He directs through darkness and light. He guides through the calm and the storm. He is in control in life and in death. He leadeth me.

[This section completed on Lord's Day, 18th September, 1966, sixtieth day of imprisonment]

3.   **THE THINGS OF THE SPIRIT**

"For they that are after the flesh do mind the things of the flesh; but they that are after the Spirit the things of the Spirit. For to be carnally minded is death; but to be spiritually minded is life and peace. Because the carnal mind is enmity against God; for it is not subject to the law of God, neither indeed can be", vs. 5, 6, 7.

In these verses we have the things of the Spirit and the spiritual mind contrasted with the things of the flesh and the carnal mind. "As he thinketh in his heart", said the scripture, "so is he" (Prov. 23:7).

(a) *The Things of the Flesh and the Carnal Mind*

Three important truths should be noted.

(1) *The Conception of the Things of the Flesh*

The carnal mind is the womb, the birthplace of the things of the flesh. The carnal mind is enmity against God and is not subject to the law of God neither indeed can be, v. 7. It cannot be transformed or regenerated into the spiritual mind. That which is born of the flesh is flesh and will forever remain flesh. The carnal mind is the mind of the old nature and the place for the old man and all his work is the cross.

(2) *The Character of the Things of the Flesh*

The character of the things of the flesh is set forth in Galatians 5:19-21.

"Now the works of the flesh are manifest, which are these, Adultery, fornication, uncleanness, lasciviousness, idolatry, witchcraft, hatred, variance, emulations, wrath, strife, seditions, heresies, envyings, murders, drunkenness, revellings, and such like."

(3) *The Conclusion of the Things of the Flesh*

The end of the things of the flesh is death. Sin when it is finished bringeth forth death. Death is separation and death in this sense is separation from God. Separation from God means torments for the soul forever more.

(b) *The Things of the Spirit and the Spiritual Mind*
Note:

(1) *The Conception of the Things of the Spirit*

As the carnal mind is the womb of the things of the flesh so the spiritual mind or the mind of the Spirit is the womb (the place of conception) of the things of the Spirit. The spiritual mind is the mind of the new nature, and cannot be altered. It cannot sin, it is the mind of that impeccable seed in the believer. It is the mind of the Divine nature of which we are made partakers. (see I John 3:9 and II Pet. 1:4). That which is born of the Spirit is spirit and will forever remain spirit.

(2) *The Character of the Things of the Spirit*

The character of the things of the Spirit is revealed in Galatians 5:22 and 23.

"But the fruit of the Spirit is love, joy, peace, longsuffering, gentleness, goodness, faith, meekness, temperance; against such there is no law".

(3) *The Conclusion of the Things of the Spirit*

"To be spiritually minded is life and peace", v. 6.

The end of the things of the Spirit is life and peace, eternal life and eternal peace.

"Finally, brethren, whatsoever things are true, whatsoever things are honest, whatsoever things are just, whatsoever things are pure, whatsoever things are lovely, whatsoever things are of good report; if there be any virtue, and if there be any praise, *think on these things*" (Phil. 4:8).

4. THE LIFE OF THE SPIRIT, vs. 8-13

This section is one of the most important in the whole chapter. The Life of the Spirit is, in fact, the life of the believer, the Spirit being what we may call the element of the believer. For example, we say that the air is the element of the bird. The air is in the bird and the bird is in the air. We say water is the element of the fish, the water is in the fish and the fish is in the water. So the Spirit is in the believer and the believer is in the Spirit, the Spirit being the element of the believer. Five great fundamentals of the Life of the Spirit are revealed in these verses.

1. The Foundation of the Life of the Spirit, v. 10.
2. The Impartation of the Life of the Spirit, v. 9.
3. The Culmination of the Life of the Spirit, v. 11.
4. The Obligation of the Life of the Spirit, vs. 12, 13.
5. The Commendation of the Life of the Spirit, v. 8.

(a) *The Foundation of the Life of the Spirit*

"And if Christ be in you, the body is dead because of sin; but the Spirit is life because of righteousness" (Rom. 8:10).

For a right interpretation of this verse we must ascertain what body Paul is referring to. Is it to the mortal body? I do not think so. The bodies of all men, whether Christ be in them or not, are dying bodies because of sin and could be said to be dead judicially. The expression "if Christ be in you" limits this to the Lord's people. Now what body is no longer living but dead in those who are indwelt by Christ? Surely "the body of this death" referred to in chapter 7, verse 24. On account of its sin this body was sentenced to die and the sentence was executed at the cross and the living Christ within the believer is the great proof that this is so. If Christ is in us, the body of this death is dead having been slain at the cross. This is the foundation of the Spirit's life within the believer, the old life concluded at the cross, the new life commenced at the resurrection. It can be easily seen that the whole chapter is a contrast between Spirit and flesh and that Paul uses body here in the sense of the flesh. Just the same way as he used flesh for the body in Romans 7:18 "For I know that in me (that is in my flesh - my body) dwelleth no good thing." With the death of the old man at the Cross, the spirit is life because of the reign of righteousness in the believer's heart. Righteousness was established by the Cross for the believer, and that righteousness is experienced in the heart by the Holy Ghost. This is life indeed, a reigning in righteousness by one Jesus Christ (Rom. 5:17). The Cross, then, is the foundation of the Life of the Spirit. It is of this foundation that Paul is speaking when he affirms; "I am crucified with Christ; nevertheless I live; yet not I, but Christ liveth in me; and the life which I now live in the flesh I live by the faith of the Son of God, who loved me and gave himself for me" (Gal. 2:20). This is the life of the Spirit.

(b) *The Impartation of the Life of the Spirit*

"But ye are not in the flesh, but in the Spirit, if so be that the Spirit of God dwell in you. Now if any man have not the Spirit of Christ, he is none of His", v. 9. The life of the Spirit is imparted by His entrance in regeneration into the believer's heart. It is impossible to be saved apart from the Holy Ghost. The old gospel hymn is simply stating scriptural theology in its lines -

> *Soon as my all I ventured,*
> *On the atoning blood.*
> *The Holy Spirit entered,*
> *And I was born of God.*

Notice carefully that the Spirit of God and the Spirit of Christ are but different titles for the one person. We are not Christians except the Holy Spirit dwells within us. It is His mighty incoming which imparts eternal life. By the first birth, the natural birth, human life is imparted to us, so by the second birth, the supernatural birth, spiritual life is imparted to us.

With Joseph Hart, we can say of the Blessed Holy Ghost,

> *"Tis thine to cleanse the heart,*
> *To sanctify the soul,*
> *To pour fresh life on every part*
> *And new create the whole."*

(c) *The Culmination of the Life of the Spirit*

"But if the Spirit of Him that raised up Jesus from the dead, dwell in you, he that raised up Christ from the dead shall also quicken your mortal bodies by his Spirit that dwelleth in you", v. 11. The Spirit of God is not only the quickener of the soul but also of the body.

The resurrection of the crucified body of our Lord Jesus Christ was by the Spirit of God. It was the Spirit who in the first instance commenced the life of that body in the Virgin's womb (Matt. 1:20). And it was the same Spirit who enlivened it again in Joseph's tomb. From among the dead, the Spirit of God brought forth the body of our Lord in mighty resurrection.

The self-same Spirit who has quickened our own souls and dwells within us, shall also in glorious resurrection, clothe these bodies in the robes of immortality and incorruptibility. By the Holy Ghost, "this corruptible shall have put on incorruption, and this mortal shall have put on immortality, then shall be brought to pass the saying that is written, Death is swallowed up in victory" (I Cor. 15:54). He who first breathed life into Adam's clay (Gen. 2:7) shall impart immortal life to our resurrected clay.

(d) *The Obligation of the Life of the Spirit*

"Therefore, brethren, we are debtors, not to the flesh, to live after the flesh. For if ye live after the flesh ye shall die; but if ye through the Spirit do mortify the deeds of the body, ye shall live," vs. 12, 13.

Our obligation is not now to the flesh but to the Spirit. The life of the Spirit obliges us to mortify the deeds of the body. These deeds, sinful deeds, have to be put to death for that is the meaning of the word, "mortify". This is done by obedience to the command of chapter 6:11, "Likewise reckon ye also yourselves to be dead indeed unto sin, but alive unto God through Jesus Christ our Lord". The Holy Spirit enables us to obey this command. By obedience, the Spirit's life is demonstrated within us and we live, really live, unto God.

(e) *The Commendation of the Life of the Spirit*

"So then they that are in the flesh cannot please God", v. 8. Life in the flesh cannot please God. The converse of this is true; Life in the Spirit pleases God. This life in the Spirit is the life of faith. "But without faith it is impossible to please Him" (Heb. 11:6).

It is the life of sacrifice, "Therefore let us offer the sacrifice of praise to God continually, that is, the fruit of our lips giving thanks to His Name. But to do good and to communicate, forget not: for with such sacrifices God is well pleased" (Heb. 13:15, 16).

Oh for the testimony of Enoch! "He had this testimony that he pleased God" (Heb. 11:5).

With a little reflection it will be seen that these first three aspects of the Holy Spirit and his operations are related.

1. The Law of the Spirit.
2. The Walk of the Spirit. } Our Regeneration
3. The Things of the Spirit.

These three are all associated with the life of the believer and are related to the believer's regeneration. They introduce us to the very heart of the chapter, the Life of the Spirit.

4. The Life of the Spirit
1. Its Foundation
2. Its Impartation
3. Its Culmination } Our Translation
4. Its Obligation
5. Its Commendation.

The life of the Spirit translates us out of the Kingdom of the flesh into the Kingdom of the Spirit. We are no longer in the flesh because of the life of the Spirit.

The next three truths are also related.

1. The Leading of the Spirit
2. The Cry of the Spirit   } Our Elevation
3. The Witness of the Spirit.

All these are associated with our relationship in the family of God.

The last three have a similar relationship -

1. The First-fruits of the Spirit
2. The Help of the Spirit   } Our Edification
3. The Mind of the Spirit.

All these are associated with our edification, our building up in faith, prayer and doctrine from the Holy Ghost.

5.   THE LEADING OF THE SPIRIT
"For as many as are led by the Spirit of God, they are the sons of God", v, 14.

We have already pointed out that these next three aspects of the work of the Holy Spirit, of which this is the first, are related. They have all to do with our sonship and position in the family of God. They set forth the proof of our relationship to God. This proof is threefold,

1. Outward, towards man "led by the Spirit"
2. Upwards, towards God, "Cry Abba Father".
3. Inward, towards self, "Witnessing with our Spirit".

Outward, Towards Men

Men cannot see our sonship in the family of God. Men can see our relationship to the commandments of God. The Spirit leads us to keep the commandments for we are under the law to Christ. These we keep not only in the letter but in the Spirit.

Let it be said and said as strongly as possible that the Holy Spirit never leads us to do contrary to the Word of God for the Word of God is the Mind of God and consequently the Mind of the Spirit. To break the clear commandments of the scripture for any reason at all is sin. It is still sin though cloaked over with a kiss - such a kiss is not a token of love but rather an Iscariot act of treason.

Those who oppose Biblical separation for example do so, they tell us, because they love their fellows, Romanists, Modernists, and Communists, and the separatists they maintain hate their fellows. Such men are found liars before God. For such as break God's clear commandments and teach men to do so are guilty of the worst form of hatred, hatred of God and truth. Someone has said, "To obey God is the highest form of love" and so it is. The Spirit leads us to let our "light so shine before men, that they may see your good works, and glorify your Father which is in heaven" (Matt. 5:16).

The Spirit-led man will be a marked man by his fellows. "Mark the perfect man and behold the upright", said the Psalmist, "for the end of that man is peace". The Spirit leads into the saint's everlasting rest.

6.   THE CRY OF THE SPIRIT
"For ye have not received the spirit of bondage again to fear; but ye have received the Spirit of adoption, whereby we cry, Abba, Father", v. 15.

Upwards Towards God

Here is the proof of our sonship Godwards.

The word translated "adoption" really means "placing as a son" or "sonship". What this "place as a son" means in its fullest manifestation is revealed in verse 23: "Waiting for the adoption, to wit, the redemption of our body" which will be our completed manifestation as the sons of God, v. 19. We will look at this more closely when we come to the section of the chapter containing verse 23.

The Spirit of adoption is, of course, the Holy Spirit and His cry to God of "Abba Father" is the proof Godward of our position as sons in the family of God. "Because ye are sons, God hath sent forth the Spirit of His Son into your hearts, crying, Abba, Father" (Gal. 4:6).

The word "abba" which is the Aramaic for father was used by the Eternal Son during the awful conflict in the garden of Gethsemane. With the bloody sweat upon His brow, the Son of God in agony cried, "Abba, Father, all things are possible unto Thee" (Mark 14:36).

Notice:

The Spirit of Adoption drives away all fear by replacing the fearful sense of our orphanhood with the comforting sense of God's Fatherhood.

"I will not leave you comfortless (lit. orphans): I will come to you" said the Lord Jesus (John 14:18).

7.   **THE WITNESS OF THE SPIRIT**
     "The Spirit Itself beareth witness with our spirit, that we are the
     children of God", v. 16.

Inwards Towards Self
     The Spirit Himself witnesseth within to our spirit that we are the children
of God. The Spirit does not witness to the body. Bodily excitements and physical
phenomena are no guarantees of the witness of the Spirit to a genuine work of
grace. The witness of the Spirit is not to flesh but to Spirit. Deep answers to deep
and Spirit to Spirit. Christ Himself gives us the authority to be called the children
of God. "But as many as received Him, to them gave He power (lit. authority) to
become the sons (lit. children) of God" (John 1:12). The Holy Spirit Himself
witnesseth to our spirits that this is so. From this witness springs the glad assur-
ance of peace with God and sins forgiven. The hymn we often sang in Sabbath
School expresses this truth simply but excellently.
"If one should ask of me how I can tell,
Glory to Jesus, I know very well!
God's Holy Spirit with mine doth agree,
Constantly witnessing - Jesus loves me."
     Every Christian has inside information to the fact of his personal salva-
tion. Note:
     (1) The witness of the Spirit is personal not general. "The Spirit Himself
witnesseth".
     (2) The witness of the Spirit is spiritual not physical. "With our spirit" not
with our body.
     (3) The witness of the Spirit is exceptional not universal. "We are the
children of God". Limited to those in Christ. (See I John 3:10 "children of God".)
     (4) The witness of the Spirit is mystical not natural. The proof outwardly
to men is the fact that I am led by the Spirit.
     The proof upwardly to God is the fact that I have the cry of the Spirit in
my heart.
     The proof inwardly to myself is the fact that I experience the witness of
the Spirit.

8.   **THE FIRST FRUIT OF THE SPIRIT**

     The first fruit (in verse 23 the original is in the singular) is of course a
harvest term. It is the first gleanings of the harvest, the token of the full ingathering.

The first-fruit then, of the spirit, is the pledge of the full ingathering, the mighty harvest to come.

(a) *The First-Fruit of the Harvest of Our Sovereignty*

"And if children then heirs; heirs of God, and joint-heirs with Christ", v. 17.

The sovereignty of the people of God in the purpose of God is a tremendous subject. God gave Adam sovereignty. "Be fruitful and multiply, and replenish the earth, and subdue it; and have dominion over the fish of the sea, and over the fowls of the air, and over every living thing that moveth upon the earth" (Gen. 1:28). Note the sovereignty God delegated to man in the words, "Have dominion".

Adam forfeited this sovereignty both for himself and his posterity and man instead of being a sovereign in the universe is a slave. In Christ for the redeemed man the sovereignty is restored in a few greater degrees than Adam ever experienced or even Satan ever exercised in his unfallen estate.

We are children of God brought into all the rights and privileges of sonship. This is what adoption really means, the child coming of age and publicly declared to be the son and initiated into all the rights of sonship and legally declared to be the heir.

We have the first-fruit of our heirship in the possession of the Holy Ghost. We are heirs of God and joint-heirs with Jesus Christ. The word translated "joint-heirs" is "one who is an heir along with another". We inherit with Christ. He cannot inherit without us. It is most certain that He will inherit. Therefore our inheriting is absolutely sure. We inherit together, we are joint-heirs. What a harvest we can expect from such a blessed first-fruit.

(b) *The First-Fruit of the Harvest of our Suffering*

"If so be that we suffer with Him, that we may be also glorified together. For I reckon that the sufferings of this present time are not worthy to be compared with the glory which shall be revealed in us", v. 17, 18.

Christ entered into His heritage by suffering. We, who enter into our heritage with Him by the same portal, are given the first-fruit of the Spirit, a token of the harvest we shall reap from "the sufferings of this present time". This harvest is defined as "the glory which shall be revealed in us". The first-fruit, which of necessity must be the same nature as the harvest, is the glory already begun within us. The way to the Crown is the path of the Cross but in the enduring of the Cross there is the glory of the coronation already begun within the soul. Suffering with

Christ is glorious. It was this first fruit of the Spirit which produced the galaxy of Christian martyrs, reformers, confessors, contenders and defenders, who endured as seeing Him who is invisible. Paul, as a man of experience, could say with confidence under the Spirit's inspiration, "For I reckon that the sufferings of this present time are not worthy to be compared with the glory which shall be revealed in us". That glory which is to be revealed in us is the glory of likeness to Christ. It has begun within us now by the first-fruit of the Spirit. "Where the Spirit of the Lord is there is liberty. But we all, with open face beholding as in a glass the glory of the Lord, are changed into the same image from glory to glory, even as by the Spirit of the Lord" (II Cor. 3:17, 18). This glory will have full fruit in the harvest of eternal glory. "It doth not yet appear what we shall be; but we know that, when He shall appear, we shall be like Him; for we shall see Him as He is" (I John 3:2). "That will be glory, be glory for me."

(c) *The First-Fruit of the Harvest of Our Salvation*, vs. 19-25
        The first-fruit of the Spirit is the first fruit of the harvest of our salvation. Salvation's harvest is incomprehensible by our limited minds and will have tremendous consequences. It will consist of,

(1) *The Transformation of our bodies*
        "And not only they, but ourselves also, which have the first fruits of the Spirit, even we ourselves groan within ourselves, waiting for the adoption, to wit, the redemption of our body", v. 23.
        The body of the believer at death is not buried but sown. It awaits the great harvest of the resurrection. "So also is the resurrection of the dead", saith the scripture. "It is sown in corruption; it is raised in incorruption. It is sown in dishonour; it is raised in glory: it is sown in weakness; it is raised in power. It is sown a natural body; it is raised a spiritual body" (I Cor. 15:42-44).
        The pangs of sin and the groan of sickness will then be forever no more. The first-fruit is the certain pledge that in this glorious harvest we shall share. So Paul concludes this section with the words, which require no exposition - "For we are saved by hope; but hope that is seen is not hope; for what a man seeth, why doth he yet hope for? But if we hope for that we see not, then do we with patience wait for it", vs. 24, 25.

(2) *Our Manifestation as the sons of God*
        "For the earnest expectation of the creature waiteth for the manifestation of the sons of God", v. 19. What an experience! It is anticipated in Ephesians 2:7,

"That in the ages to come He might shew the exceeding riches of His grace in His kindness toward us through Christ Jesus". What a thrill when we sit down with Christ in His throne even as He also overcame and is sat down with His father in His throne! What eternal majesty! What undiminishable glory! What infinite bliss!

(3) *The Emancipation of creation*

"For the creature was made subject to vanity, not willingly, but by reason of Him who hath subjected the same in hope. Because the creature itself also shall be delivered from the bondage of corruption into the glorious liberty of the children of God. For we know that the whole creation groaneth and travaileth in pain together until now", vs. 20-22.

The whole creation is to share in our glory. The creature subjected to bondage through sin shall escape the imprisonment of the fall. The groans of the universe will cease and the glory of the new heaven and new earth will burst forth in all the splendour of the Divine handiwork. The liberty of the glory of the sons of God (the literal reading of the last words of verse 21) will be shared by all creation.

9.   THE INTERCESSION OF THE SPIRIT

"Likewise the Spirit also helpeth our infirmities; for we know not what we should pray for as we ought; but the Spirit Itself maketh intercession for us with groanings which cannot be uttered", v. 26.

We are still in the body which is not yet transformed and we suffer many infirmities. These would overcome us and we would faint. There is however a Divine preventative to fainting. "Men ought always to pray and not to faint" (Luke 18:1). "But they that wait upon the Lord shall renew their strength; they shall mount up with wings as eagles; they shall run, and not be weary; and they shall walk, and not faint" (Isa. 40:31).

We need to pray and yet are unable of ourselves to pray. There is Divine help for us and there is a Divine intercessor within us to plead our cause, even the Holy Spirit, Himself.

(1) *His Divine Enablement*

"helpeth our infirmities". He deals with our weakness.

(2) *His Divine Enlightenment*

"We know not what we should pray for as we ought". He deals with our ignorance.

(3) *His Divine Encouragement*

"The Spirit Itself maketh intercession." He deals with our insufficiency.

Notice the three groanings,

(1) *The Creation Groans*, v. 22.

(2) *The Christian Groans*, v. 23.

(3) *The Comforter Groans*, v. 26.

Through the groaning of the Comforter both the Christian and the creation will cease from groaning and experience full transformation.

10. THE MIND OF THE SPIRIT

"And He that searcheth the hearts knoweth what is the mind of the Spirit, because He maketh intercession for the saints according to the will of God", v. 27.

The mind of the Spirit leads us into a penetration of the "all things" of God We are led to know the mind of the Spirit in the verses which follow verse 27.

"And we know that all things work together for good to them that love God, to them who are the called according to His purpose", v. 28. The "all things" of this text has often been taken in the widest possible sense. Doubtless, God in His sovereignty pieces all things of life together for our good. Certainly "He doeth according to His will in the army of heaven, and among the inhabitants of the earth; and none can stay His hand, or say unto Him, Who doest Thou?" (Dan. 4:35).

The "all things" in our text however can be clearly defined. If we look at verse 31 we have the question, "What shall we then say to these things?" The "all things" are the "these things". What things? The great eternal truths of verses 29 and 30.

"For whom He did foreknow, He also did predestinate to be conformed to the image of His Son, that He might be the firstborn among many brethren. Moreover whom he did predestinate, them He also called; and whom He called, them He also justified; and whom He justified, them He also glorified".

(a) *Our Being foreknown by God*

"Whom He did foreknow".

Here we have revealed the eternal thoughts of the mind of the Spirit.

Let it be said and said as strongly as possible that this does not say that God foresaw that a certain number of people would believe and having forseen their faith elected them to everlasting salvation. Those who read the text thus are guilty of adding to God's Word. Nothing is left to chance. God sees what is going to happen, because He planned it so. His foreknowledge rests on His foreordination. How otherwise would the scripture be true? "Who worketh all things after the counsel of His own will" (Eph. 1:11).

What then does foreknow in the text mean? Knowledge in the Bible is often simply acquaintance with a person, e.g., John "was known unto the high priest" (John 18:15). Knowledge is also intimate knowledge, a knowledge of depth, e.g., Paul said that "I may know Him" (Phil. 3:10). Knowledge is sometimes used as the knowledge of the marriage union, the knowledge of love, e.g., "Adam knew Eve his wife". This is its strongest use. We could say, Adam loved Eve his wife. I believe that foreknowledge here is used in its strongest sense and has force of foreloving. Whom He did forelove (carrying within in the meaning of both personal acquaintance and intimate knowledge) is the real meaning of the text. This foreloving is one of the eternal thoughts of the mind of the Spirit.

(b) *On Being Predestinated by God*

"He also did predestinate to be conformed to the image of His Son, that He might be the first-born among many brethren."

Predestination is appointing our destiny beforehand. This destiny we have already seen in verses 19-25. It consists of (a) the transforming of our bodies, (b) our manifestation as the sons of God, (c) the emancipation of creation. Here it is described in the tremendous words, "conformed to the image of His Son" and then the eternal thought in the mind of the Spirit prompting it all is revealed, "that He might be the first-born among many brethren" the enlargement of the family in and for the fellowship of His Son.

The expression "first-born" is worthy of special attention.

Christ is the first-born of the Virgin (Luke 2:7) - that establishes *His Purity*.

Christ is the first-born among his brethren (Rom. 8:29) - that establishes *His Primacy*.

Christ is the first-born from among the dead (Col. 1:18) - that establishes *His Potency*.

Christ is the first-born of every creature (Col 1:15) - that establishes *His Pre-eminency*.

(c) *On being called of God*

"Them He also called".

Bunyan in the second part of *The Pilgrim's Progress* tells of a scene in the House of the Interpreter - the hen with her four calls.

(1) She hath a common call, and that she hath all the day long.

(2) She hath a special call, and that she had but sometimes.

(3) She had a brooding call, and

(4) She had an outcry" (Matt 23:37).

"Now," said he (the Master of the house), "compare this hen to your King, and these chickens to His obedient ones. For, answerable to her, Himself has His methods, which He walketh in towards His people; by His common call, He gives nothing; by His special call, He always has something to give; He has also a brooding voice, for them that are under His wings; and He has an outcry to give the alarm when He seeth the enemy come." The calling in the verse is the special calling of grace, the effectual calling of the gospel.

"He drew me, and I followed on,

Charmed to confess the voice Divine."

It is the mind of the Spirit to call us to Himself.

(d) *On Being Justified*

"Them He also justified".

The mind of the Spirit on this great truth we have already seen in the previous chapters of the epistle.

"No hope can on the law be built

of justifying grace;

That law that shows the sinner's guilt,

condemns him to his face.

Jesus! how glorious is thy grace!

When in thy name we trust,

Our faith receives a righteousness

that makes the sinner just."

(e) *On Being Glorified*

"Them He also glorified".

The mind of the Spirit has been revealed on the subject of our glorification in verses 19-25

"The men of grace have found
Glory begun below;
Celestial fruits on earthly ground
From faith and hope may grow.

"The hill of Zion yields
A thousand sacred sweets,
Before we reach the heavenly fields
Or walk the golden streets.

"There shall we see His face,
And never, never sin;
There from the rivers of His grace,
Drink endless pleasures in."

~ Isaac Watts 1674-1748.

We learn from these things, five great truths concerning the things of God.

THE ANSWER TO FIVE QUESTIONS, vs. 31-39

In answer to the question, "What shall we then say to these things?" Paul asks five other questions and in their asking also gives the answer.

The First Answer - God's Person is Invincible
"If God be for us, who can be against us", v. 31.

God's is invincible. The "who" of opposition is not worthy of even a thought if such a God is for us. If Divinity is for us, shall we fear all combined humanity?

If Omnipotence is for us, shall we fear amalgamated impotence?

If heaven is for us, shall we fear united hell?

"Hast thou not known? hast thou not heard, that the everlasting God, the Lord, the Creator of the ends of the earth, fainteth not, neither is weary? there is no searching of His understanding. He giveth power to the faint; and to them that have no might He increaseth strength" (Isa. 40:28, 29).

The Second Answer - God's Grace is Exhaustible
"He that spared not His own Son, but delivered Him up for us all, how shall He not with Him also freely give us all things?", v. 32.

(1) *God's Grace is inexhaustible in its Mystery*

"He that spared not His own Son".

The Bible tells us that God "spared not" the old world but poured His wrath upon the universe (II Pet. 2:5). It also tells us that God "spared not" the angels who sinned but destroyed one third of the celestial race (II Pet. 2:4, Rev. 12:4).

It further tells us that God "spared not unbelieving Israel but judged even the chosen race for their awful sin of rejecting His Son (Rom. 11:21). We can understand something of the justice of these "spared nots". But when we read that God "spared not His own Son", this is grace inexhaustible in its mystery.

(2) *God's Grace is inexhaustible in its Miracle*

"But delivered Him up for us all".

To give His Son for angels we might understand, but to give Him for me, that's the inexhaustible miracle of grace.

> *"How amazing God's compassion,*
> *That so vile a worm might prove,*
> *This stupendous bliss of heaven,*
> *This amazing wealth of love."*

He loved me and gave Himself for me (Gal. 2:20).

(3) *God's Grace is inexhaustible in its Magnitude*

"How shall He not with Him also freely give us all things?"

God's grace is inexhaustible in its magnitude. With His Son God freely gives us all things.

"All are yours; and ye are Christ's and Christ is God's" (I Cor 3:22, 23).

The Third Answer - God's Verdict is Incontrovertible

"Who shall lay anything to the charge of God's elect? It is God that justifieth", v. 33.

The infinite God justifies; the eternal God justifies; the unchangeable God justifies. He justifies in wisdom, in power, in holiness, in justice, in goodness and truth.

This verdict is incontrovertible. The elect are cleared forever.

> *"What though the accuser roar,*
> *of ills that I have done.*
> *I know them well and thousands more,*
> *Jehovah findeth none."*

The Fourth Answer - God's Pardon is Incontestable
"Who is He that condemneth? It is Christ that died, yea, rather, that is risen again, who is even at the right hand of God. Who also can make intercession for us", v, 34.

Can *Christ's substitution* be contested? "It is Christ that died.

Can *Christ's supplication* be contested? "Who also maketh risen again".

Can *Christ's sovereignty* be contested? "Who is even at the right hand of God."

Can *Christ's supplication* be contested? "Who also maketh intercession for us."

The Fifth Answer - God's Bond is Inseparable
"Who shall separate us from the love of Christ? Shall tribulation, or distress, or persecution, or famine, or nakedness, or peril, or sword? As it is written, For thy sake, we are killed all the day long; we are accounted as sheep for the slaughter. Nay, in all these things we are more than conquerors through Him that loved us", vs. 35-37.

"For I am persuaded, that neither death, nor life, nor angels, nor principalities, nor powers, nor things present, nor things to come, nor height, nor depth, nor any other creature, shall be able to separate us from the love of God, which is in Christ Jesus our Lord", vs 38, 39.

It can be easily seen that there are two sets of circumstances which Paul lists in these verses.

(1) *The circumstances before Death*, vs. 35-37
There are seven of these:

(1) Tribulation,
(2) Distress,
(3) Persecution,
(4) Famine,
(5) Nakedness,
(6) Peril,
(7) Sword.

Seven is one of the scripture numbers of completion and perfection.[2] The complete onslaught of every foe before death cannot separate us from the love of

God. God's bond is inseparable before death. "Nay, in all these things we are more than conquerors."

(2) The Circumstances after Death, vs. 38, 39.

There are ten of these. Ten is another number of scripture standing for completion and perfection. That is the life mentioned here is life after death comes first. If it were this life it would of course be mentioned first and then be followed by death.

(1) Death - death itself with all its terrors and triumph.

(2) Life - the life after death with all its mysterious reality.

(3) Angels - the inhabitants of heaven, the Celestial Forces.

(4) Principalities ⎫ the inhabitants of hell, the Satanic Forces.
(5) Powers   ⎭

(6) Things Present - The content of our life on earth. Our works follow us.

(7) Things to Come - The content of eternity.

(8) Height - The heights of heaven.

(9) Depth - The depths of hell.

(10 Any other creature - Created thing in original. Anything else in the great beyond. None of these, the complete circumstance after death, "shall be able to separate us from the love of God, which is in Christ Jesus our Lord." God's bond is inseparable after death.

> "Who then can e'er divide us more,
>   from Jesus and His Love,
> Or break the sacred chain that binds,
>   the earth to heaven above.

> "Let troubles rise, and terrors frown,
>   and days of darkness fall;
> Through Him all dangers we'll defy,
>   and more than conquer all.

> "Nor death, nor life, nor earth, nor hell,
>   nor time's destroying sway,
> Can e'er efface us from His heart,
>   or make His love decay.

"Each future period that will bless,
as it has bless'd the past;
He lov'd us from the first of time,
He loves us to the last."

Amen and Amen.

[This section completed on the sixty-seventh day of imprisonment:
Lord's Day, 25th September, 1966]

Footnotes

1. I write this in my prison cell on Saturday, 17th September, being 59 days in prison and I cannot refrain from shouting a loud, "Hallelujah!"

2. The Hebrew word for seven is derived from the verb meaning "to be full", "to be satisfied", "to have enough of".

    On the seventh day God rested from His creative work. It was complete, it required no additions.

    The number seven marks off the days of the week and the seven-day week is universal and immemorial in its observance in all times and by all nations.

    It completes the number of notes in the scale, the eighth is only the repetition of the first. It completes the colours of the spectrum and rainbow.

    The first verse of the Bible in the Hebrew has but seven words (Gen. 1:1).

    It is interesting to note that some words, very characteristic of heaven, occur but seven times in the New Testament "Zion", "a kiss", "a song" and "a psalm".

9 The principle of
Sovereign Grace

CHAPTERS NINE, TEN and eleven are closely related. They unfold some of the profoundest aspects of God's sovereignty and grace, each having as a common background the people of Israel.

In chapter nine we have the Principle of Grace.

In chapter ten we have the Preaching of Grace.

In chapter eleven we have the Purpose of Grace.

It is grace triumphant in every chapter.

In chapter nine the Principle of Gace triumphs in Election.

In chapter ten the Preaching of Grace triumphs in Salvation.

In chapter eleven the Purpose of Grace triumphs in Restoration.

THE PRINCIPLE OF GRACE GOD'S SOVEREIGNTY IN ELECTION

This chapter has five sections. Each of these sections sets forth a great fact about Election.

(1) Election - No deterrent to the passion for souls.

(2) Election - Not decided by natural causes - Foreseen or otherwise.

(3) Election - Never decreed in unrighteousness.

(4) Election - Not determined by national circumstances.

(5) Election - Not demonstrated by the words of the law.

1.   **ELECTION, NO DETERRENT TO THE PASSION FOR SOULS**
**"I say the truth in Christ, I lie not, my conscience also bearing me
witness in the Holy Ghost, that I have great heaviness and continual sorrow in my heart. For I could wish that myself were accursed from Christ for my brethren, my kinsmen according to
the flesh; who are Israelites; to whom pertaineth the adoption,
and the glory, and the covenants, and the giving of the law, and
the service of God, and the promises; whose are the fathers, and
of whom as concerning the flesh Christ came, who is over all,
God blessed for ever. Amen", vs. 1-5.**

What God reveals in His Book we accept. We bow to the authority of Holy
Scripture. We come to the Word of God, to be taught. However unpleasing to
the natural mind the revealed truth of God may be, we acknowledge its supreme
rulership. Our task is not to question, our duty is rather to accept and obey.

The doctrine of election, like the Elect One Himself (i.e. our Lord Jesus
Christ, Isaiah 42:1), is a stumbling stone and rock of offence to many. The pride of
man is smashed forever on this eternal granite of Divine glory. "Whosoever shall
fall upon that stone shall be broken; but on whomsoever it shall fall, it will grind
him to powder" (Luke 20:18).

Let it be said, however, and said once and for all that election does not
destroy the responsibility of second causes.

When man seeks to escape from his responsibilities by making a plea of
God's sovereignty, his view of God's sovereignty is fallacious.

How often has the doctrine of unconditional election been argued against
in this way. "If election is true then I don't need to pray, to plead and to preach. I
couldn't believe this doctrine, it would rob me of my incentive in God's work."

Evidently the incentive in such a case must be human and not divine.

How refreshing it is to turn to the plain statements of God's Word and
bow without argument before the sole arbiter of faith and practice.

The first few verses in this chapter show plainly that election is no different to the passion for souls. Standing at the very portal of this tremendous chapter on unconditional election they give the lie to all who would say otherwise.

Five characteristics of Paul's Passion for Souls are revealed in these first
five verses.

(a) *The Verity of Paul's Passion*
"I say the truth"; "I lie not"; "my conscience also bearing me witness", v. 1.

Paul's passion for souls was no make-believe. He is speaking here the words of truth and soberness. His sincerity and verity shine forth clearly and plainly in his honest speech. "I say the truth", he declares. "I lie not", he affirms. "My conscience also bearing me witness", he exclaims. Paul is in deadly earnest and his life work is proof positive of the verity of his passion for souls. He dwarfs the modern preachers to pygmy size by his giant ministry.

"Are they ministers of Christ? (I speak as a fool) I am more; in labours more abundant, in stripes above measure, in prisons more frequent, in deaths oft. Of the Jews five times received I forty stripes save one (195 altogether). Thrice was I beaten with rods, once was I stoned, thrice I suffered shipwreck, a night and a day I have been in the deep; in journeyings often, in perils of waters, in perils of robbers, in perils by mine own countrymen, in perils by the heathen, in perils in the city, in perils in the wilderness, in perils in the sea, in perils among the false brethren; in weariness and painfulness, in watchings often, in hunger and thirst, in fastings often, in cold and nakedness. Beside those things that are without, that which cometh upon me daily, the care of all the churches. Who is weak, and I am not weak. who is offended, and I burn not? If I must needs glory, I will glory of the things which concern mine infirmities. The God and Father of our Lord Jesus Christ, which is blessed for evermore, knoweth that I lie not" (II Cor. 11:23-32).

(b) *The Divinity of Paul's Passion*

"In Christ". "In the Holy Ghost", v. 1.

This passion of Paul's heart was Divine. This was no emotional flare-up. This flame was ignited at the fires of the burning heart of the Christ of the cross and constantly fed by the oil of God the Holy Ghost. It was such a partaking of the passion of Christ that it enabled Paul to declare that he was able "to fill up that which is behind of the afflictions of Christ in my flesh for His (Christ's) body's sake, which is the church" (Col. 1:24).

(c) *The Reality of Paul's Passion*

"That I have great heaviness and continual sorrow in my heart", v. 2.

Paul demonstrated the reality of the passion by the burden of his soul. He bore a heaviness which led to a continual sorrow. From this there was no escape. Deep sorrow filled his soul, his thoughts and his mind. Heaviness was the constant experience of his life. He was a burdened man. His passion for souls was real.

140 **An Exposition of the** *Epistle to the Romans*

(d) *The Intensity of Paul's Passion*

"For I could wish that myself were accursed from Christ", v. 3.

The intensity of the passion is seen in these tremendous words; not that I wish myself accursed but that I *could* wish myself accursed from Christ. Here Paul is going with Christ through the garden and right on to the cross. Here is fellowship with Christ in His sufferings. The word accursed is a very strong word. We could read it as "damned from Christ". What intensity! that could wish to be in hell for the salvation of others. Of this flame let my own soul be ignited.

(e) *The Affinity of Paul's Passion*

It was for his own people that he prayed and longed after in the bowels of Christ (Phil 1:8).

Note:

(1) *Their Position* - "my brethren, my kinsmen according to the flesh", v. 3.

(2) *Their Privilege* - "Who are Israelites; to whom pertaineth the adoption, and the glory, and the covenants, and the giving of the law, and the service of God, and the promises", v. 4.

(3) *Their Pedigree* - "Whose are the fathers", v. 5.

"Concerning the flesh Christ came, who is over all, God blessed forever. Amen", v. 5.

What a declaration!

(1) *Christ's Humanity* - "Concerning the flesh Christ came".

(2) *Christ's Authority* - "Who is over all".

(3) *Christ's Deity* - "God blessed forever. Amen".

No wonder the modern infidel translators attack this verse so consistently and seek to evacuate it of its precious truth!

We learn then that election is no deterrent to the Passion for souls.

2. ELECTION - NOT DECIDED BY NATURAL CAUSES, FORSEEN OR OTHERWISE, vs. 6-13

We have already pointed out when expounding the twenty-ninth verse of the eighth chapter what election is not - God looking into the future and because He foresees something that is to happen He then foreordains that particular happening. For example, He foresees those who will believe, it is argued, and He therefore elects them to eternal life. This argument is unscriptural and does not expound Biblical election. The Bible teaches plainly that God foreknows because

He has foreordained. Nothing is left to chance. Our God is sovereign for if He were not sovereign He would not be God. The great truth of Unconditional Election is declared in these verses with great plainness of speech.

(a) *The Elect Seed*

"Not as though the word of God hath taken none effect. For they are not all Israel, which are of Israel. Neither, because they are the seed of Abraham, are they all children; but in Isaac shall thy seed be called. That is, they which are the children of the flesh, these are not the children of God; but the children of the promise are counted for the seed. For this is the word of promise. At this time will I come, and Sarah shall have a son", vs. 6-9.

Natural causes have nothing whatsoever to do with election. Election is an act of God governed only and solely by His good pleasure. Abraham was the father of many sons, Ishmael by Hagar, Isaac by Sarah and Zimran. Jokshan, Medon, Mediau, Isbak and Shuah by Keturah. These were all the sons of Abraham and of his seed, yet were they not all the children of promise. For they are not all Israel which are of Israel, v. 6.

It was Isaac the son of Sarah who was the elect seed and the child of promise. The sovereign Lord said, "In Isaac shall thy seed be called" and that was the matter eternally settled. The decision in election is solely and absolutely the Lord's. Natural circumstances do not decide the matter whether those circumstances are foreseen or not.[1]

(b) *The Elect Son*

"And not only this; but when Rebecca also conceived by one, even by our father Isaac; (for the children being not yet born, neither having done any good or evil, that the purpose of God according to election might stand, not of works, but of Him that calleth). It was said unto her, The elder shall serve the younger. As it is written, Jacob have I loved, but Esau I have hated", vs. 10-13.

Mark, moral character does not decide election. Two sons were to be born to Isaac. A great struggle took place in Rebekah's womb. Before the sons were born God told her that "two nations are in thy womb, and two manner of people shall be separated from thy bowels; and the one people shall be stronger than the other people; and the elder shall serve the younger" (Gen. 25:23). The choice was made then before the moral characters of the sons were known. The choice is solely and absolutely Divine. "As it is written, Jacob have I loved, Esau have I hated" (see Malachi 1:2, 3). Jacob was the elect son for that was the purpose, not of man, nor of flesh nor of blood, but of God.

So it is made unmistakably clear that Election is not decided by natural causes, forseen or otherwise.

3.   ELECTION - NEVER DECREED IN UNRIGHTEOUSNESS, vs. 14-24

Immediately unconditional election is declared the natural man will question its righteousness.

What shall we then say? Is there unrighteousness with God? God forbid, v. 14.

Paul answers the cavil of proud man in a threefold argument (a) by the Revelation to the Prophet (b) by the Demonstration in the Pharaoh, and (c) by the Illustration about the Potter.

(a) *The Revelation to the Prophet*

"For He saith to Moses, I will have mercy on whom I will have mercy, and I will have compassion on whom I will have compassion. So then it is not of him that willeth, or of him that runneth, but of God that sheweth mercy" vs. 15, 16.

What God says is always right and always righteous. Righteousness is not something measured by the standard of man's opinion; righteousness is established by the word of God. God always acts in a righteous manner. His ways are the ways of righteousness. His Word is the word of righteousness. His law is the law of righteousness. His purpose is the purpose of righteousness. His throne is the throne of righteousness. His acts are the acts of righteousness. His choice is the choice of righteousness. To His prophet Moses, he revealed that righteousness depended on his "I will" (Exod. 33:19). What God calls wills is righteousness. If He wills to have mercy that is righteous mercy. If He wills to harden that is righteous judgment. Election in righteousness depends not on the will of man, for it is not of him that willeth, not on the works of man, for it depends not on him that runneth but on the mercy of God for it depends on God that sheweth mercy.

(b) *The Demonstration in the Pharaoh*

"For the scripture saith unto Pharaoh. Even for this same purpose have I raised thee up, that I might shew My power in thee, and that My name might be declared throughout all the earth. Therefore hath He mercy on whom He will have mercy, and whom He will he hardeneth", vs. 17, 18.

Election was demonstrated in the life of Pharaoh the tyrant.

Election did not in the least iota lessen Pharaoh's responsibility. Pharaoh was morally responsible for hardening his own heart. He deliberately and persistently refused to let Israel go from under his slavery. In Exodus, 8:15, 32 and (:34, 35, we read that he sinned and wilfully hardened his heart.

Yet to Pharaoh God could say by Moses, "And in very deed for this cause have I raised thee up, for to shew in thee My power; and that My name may be declared throughout all the earth" (Exod. 9:16).

Who would, after reading the record, dare to challenge God with unrighteousness in his judgment of Pharaoh? Mark the conclusion of this demonstration, "Therefore hath He (God) mercy on whom He will have mercy, and whom He will He hardeneth", v. 18.

(c) *The Illustration about the Potter*

"Thou wilt say then unto me, Why doth He yet find fault. For who hath resisted His will? Nay but, O man, who art thou that rebellest against God? Shall the thing formed say to him that formed it, Why hast thou made me thus. Hath not the potter power over the clay, of the same lump to make one vessel unto honour, and another unto dishonour? What if God, willing to shew His wrath, and to make His power known, endured with much long-suffering the vessels of wrath fitted to destruction; and that He might make known the riches of His glory on the vessel of mercy, which He has afore prepared unto glory. Even us, whom He hath called, not of the Jews only, but also of the Gentiles?" vs. 19-24.

Paul answers this cavil of the natural man with the question, "Shall the thing formed say to him that formed it, why hast thou made me thus?" v. 20. He then takes for an illustration the potter and the clay. (Proud man needs to be reminded that he is but clay.) The authority of the potter is sovereign and there is no unrighteousness with him no matter what vessel he fashions. So it is with God. Vessels of wrath fitted for destruction or vessels of mercy afore prepared for glory are both eternal monuments of his righteousness. The will of God is supreme and supremely righteous.

4.   ELECTION - NOT DETERMINED BY NATIONAL CIRCUMSTANCES
"As He saith also in Osee, I will call them my people, which were not my people; and her beloved, which was not beloved. And it shall come to pass, that in the place where it was said unto them, Ye are not my people; there shall they be called the children of the living God. Esaias also crieth concerning Israel. Though

the number of the children of Israel be as the sand of the sea, a
remnant shall be saved. For He will finish the work, and cut it
short in righteousness; because a short work will the Lord make
upon the earth. And as Esaias said before, Except the Lord of Sabbath had left us a seed, we had been as Sodom and been made
like unto Gomorrha", vs. 25-29.

The Jews thought that election was their privilege and their privilege alone.
They concluded that it was based on fleshly pedigree. They were convinced that
it was a racial blessing reserved only for them. Paul takes the Jews up on this very
argument and with their own scriptures he shows plainly that this is not so. He
quotes at length from Hosea 2:23 and 1:10 and from Isaiah 10:22 and 23 and 1:9
to prove his point that election is not determined by national circumstances. The
principle of grace and of grace alone determines our election of God.

5.   ELECTION - NOT DEMONSTRATED BY THE WORKS OF THE LAW
"What shall we say then? That the Gentiles, which followed not
after righteousness, have attained to righteousness, even the righteousness which is of faith. But Israel, which followed after the
law of righteousness, hath not attained to the law of righteousness. Wherefore? Because they sought it not by faith, but as it
were by the works of the law. For they stumbled at that stumbling stone; As it is written, Behold I lay in Sion a stumbling stone
and rock of offence; and whosoever believeth on Him shall not be
ashamed", vs. 30-33.

The righteousness of faith alone is the demonstration of genuine election. This faith is also the gift of God (Eph. 2:8, 9), "for all men have not faith" (II
Thess. 3:2). Israel by seeking to justify themselves by the law of righteousness
demonstrated their reprobation rather than their predestination. They thus "stumbled at that stumbling stone; As it is written, Behold I lay in Sion a stumbling
stone and rock of offence; and whosoever believeth on Him shall not be ashamed",
vs. 32, 33.

[This section completed on the sixty-ninth day of imprisonment:
Tuesday, 27th September, 1966]

Footnotes
1.   We would heartily commend to our readers CH Spurgeon's great sermon entitled "Election".

10 The preaching of *Sovereign Grace*

IN CHAPTER NINE we have the principle of grace vindicated; now in chapter ten we have the preaching of grace delineated.

1.   THE PREREQUISITE OF THE PREACHING
"Brethren, my heart's desire and prayer to God for Israel is, that they might be saved. For I bear them record that they have a zeal of God, but not according to knowledge. For they being ignorant of God's righteousness, and going about to establish their own righteousness, have not submitted themselves unto the righteousness of God", vs. 1-3.

Three great prerequisites to preaching the gospel are declared in these verses.

(a) *The Experience of the Passion for Souls*
"my heart's desire".
Preaching is not a matter of the head but rather of the heart. Salvation results from heart belief, "With the heart man believeth unto righteousness", v. 10. In order to reach the hearts of his hearers the preacher must first have his own

heart reached. In order to move the hearts of his hearer the preacher's heart itself must first be moved. In order to break the hearts of his hearers the preacher must first himself experience a broken heart. Head preaching can only reach the head but preaching from the heart will reach the heart. The gospel does not aim at mere intellectual conversion, the gospel aims at heart regeneration.

The preacher's message can only catch real converting fire in the passion of his own heart. Passionless preaching is the bane of both pulpit and pew. Without passion the preacher is only the vain sound of religious brass and the useless tinkling of ecclesiastical cymbals. The heart of the preacher must be right if he is to set right the hearts of his hearers. Without the flame of passion the preacher is as useless as the pulpit in which he stands - so much dead wood.

John Wesley's advice to the critic of the preacher was right. "Pray that God will set your minister on fire and the people will come out to see him burn." Aye, and the people will catch the fire, for fire spreads. Well might CH Spurgeon exclaim, "If there's a fireman in the pulpit there'll be no snowmen in the pews!"

Paul's heart burned and blazed with an unceasing desire to save the lost. In season and out of season this fire still burned. Oh for a similar desire to captivate my soul! Oh to be imprisoned with this one overwhelming passion!

(b) *The Employment of the Prayer of Faith*

"Prayer to God for Israel is that they might be saved", v. 1.

Before the preacher can talk to men about God he must talk to God about men. Prayer is one of the great prerequisites of preaching. Without prayer, preaching is a mere useless religious performance like the laying of the prophet's staff on the dead child's form and results in neither voice nor hearing (I Kings 4:31). Prayerless preaching is powerless to beget life.

The secret of preaching is prayer, a secret too well known but alas little availed of. Luther instructed his students aright when he taught them, "He that has prayed well has studied well".

Prayerlessness is the Achan in the camp of God. Prayerlessness is the leprous Miriam in the house of the High Priest. Prayerlessness is the Absalom among the King's sons. Prayerlessness is the great sin of the Church and the great curse of my own heart. The sin of prayerlessness must be confessed, cleansed and forsaken in the preacher's life. Otherwise he cannot successfully preach the gospel of Sovereign Grace.

Prayer is employment, it is the task of prayer. Prayer is worship, it is "to God" that we pray.

Prayer is intercession, it was "for Israel" Paul prayed.

Prayer is petition, it was for the salvation of Israel that Paul prayed.

Oh to excel in this happy employment, holy worship, heavenly intercession and humble petition!

(c) *The Estimation of the Plight of Man* vs. 2, 3

Paul had a clear estimation of the plight of those for whom he prayed. Such an estimation is a prerequisite for preaching. If the preacher is not overwhelmed with the desperate need of his hearers his preaching will lack the vital potency.

(1) *Their Zealousness*

"For I bear them record that they have a zeal for God, but not according to knowledge", v. 2.

Paul saw the zeal of Israel but alas it was not according to knowledge. It was even a zeal of God yet it was vain for it was misdirected. Have we, as believers, estimated properly the tragedy of the misdirected zeal of Romanists and other false religionists? Has a consideration of their ignorant zeal moved us with compassion for the salvation of their souls? Have we really considered the vanity and folly of their misdirected zeal?

(2) *Their Self-righteousness*

"For they being ignorant of God's righteousness, and going about to establish their own righteousness", v. 3. Paul had a clear estimation of the self-righteousness of Israel. It commenced in an ignorance of what God's righteousness really is. It culminated in a self-righteousnesses which was only a cloak of perdition. "But we are all as an unclean thing, for all our righteousness are as filthy rags; and we all do fade as a leaf; and our iniquities, like the wind, have taken us away" (Isa. 64:6).

Do we truly estimate the ignorance of sinners? How blind they are to god's truth! How they work to establish a rotten self-righteousness which will bring them into greater damnation! Oh the utter folly of religion without Christ our righteousness!

> *"Not the labour of my hands,*
> *Can fulfil Thy law's demands;*
> *Could my zeal no respite know,*
> *Could my tears forever flow,*
> *All for sin could not atone,*
> *Thou must save and thou alone".*
>
> ~ A.M .Toplady, 1740-1778.

(3) *Their Stubbornness*

"Have not submitted themselves unto the righteousness of God", v. 3.

Israel would not submit themselves unto the righteousness of God. They fought against Christ, the Lord our Righteousness, and rejected Him as their promised Messiah. They became rebels and warred against their God. Refusing to go His way, in their stubbornness, they went to hell.

Clear views of the plight of man in his sinful stubbornness against God's way of salvation are very necessary for the faithful and effectual preaching of the gospel of sovereign grace. Before we can really preach grace as high as heaven we must realise the need is as deep as hell.

2.   THE PROCLAMATION OF THE PREACHING, vs. 4-8

The great proclamation of the preaching is Christ. The preaching of the gospel of Sovereign Grace is the preaching of Christ and the glorious truth that grace and truth came by Him to us (John 1:17). Notice the order, grace first. If truth had come first we would have perished. But grace preceded truth thus preparing us not for its knowledge unto our condemnation but rather for its knowledge unto our emancipation, for "ye shall know the truth, and the truth shall make you free" (John 8:32).

"For Moses described the righteousness which is of the law. That the man which doeth those things shall live by them", v. 5, Cp. Leviticus 18:5 and Nehemiah 9:29. These words of Moses cast a despairing gloom over all mankind. The commandments from Sinai's flaming peak no man is able to perform. They are a burden which no man can carry and a bondage no son of Adam can endure. In the village of Morality under the patronage of Mr Legality the burdened sinner will only find greater condemnation. The answer to the sinner's need is not Moses but Christ, not the law but grace and not Sinai but Calvary, Christ in a threefold aspect must be presented.

(a) *The Accomplishing Christ*

"For Christ is the end of the law for righteousness to everyone that believeth", v. 4. What we could not accomplish for ourselves Christ has accomplished for us. Christ in all the accomplishing of His virgin birth, virtuous life, vicarious death and victorious resurrection is the grand subject of gospel preaching. The great object of Christ's life and work on the Cross was the providing of righteousness for everyone that believeth.

Christ is the end of the law. Place Him at the end of every commandment of the law for He is the complete fulfilment of them all. Place Him at the end of every precept of the law for He is the complete accomplishment of them all. Place Him at the end of every requirement of the law for He is the complete perfection of them all. Place Him at the end of every type of the law for He is the great arch-type of them all.

He is the accomplishing Christ for He has accomplished justifying righteousness not only for all who have believed but also for all who will yet believe. Upon His glorious finished work I depend for all eternity.

> *Behold the Saviour on the Cross,*
> *A spectacle of woe!*
> *See from His agonising wounds*
> *The blood incessant flow;*
> *Till death's pale ensigns o'er His cheek*
> *And trembling lips were spread;*
> *Till light forsook His closing eyes,*
> *And life His drooping head!*
>
> *'Tis finished - was His latest voice;*
> *These sacred accents o'er*
> *He bowed His head, gave up the ghost,*
> *And suffered pain no more.*
> *'Tis finished - the Messiah dies,*
> *for sins but not His own;*
> *The great redemption is complete,*
> *And Satan's power o'er thrown.*
>
> *'Tis finished - all His groans are past;*
> *His blood, His pain and toils,*
> *Have fully vanquished our foes,*
> *And crowned Him with their spoils.*
> *'Tis finished - legal worship ends,*
> *And gospel ages run;*
> *All old things now are passed away,*
> *And a new world begun.*
>
> ~ Paraphrase 44.

(b) *The Available Christ*

"But the righteousness which is of faith speaketh on this wise, Say not in thine heart, Who shall ascend into heaven? (that is, to bring Christ down from above); Or, Who shall descend into the deep? (that is to bring up Christ again from the dead)," vs. 6, 7.

The accomplishing Christ is the Available Christ to sinners. He is available now to all who will call upon Him. The basic error of all the "isms" is that the Christ whom they present is not immediately available to the sinner. He is hedged around by religious traditions and man-made ordinances and is thus far removed from needy sinners. The Christ proclaimed in the gospel is the available Christ, available to the sinner in his dire need. Christ is Emmanuel, God is with us.

(c) *The Accessible Christ*

"But what saith it? The word is nigh thee, even in thy mouth, and in thy heart; that is, the word of faith, which we preach", v. 8.

The remedy to a disease may be available but not accessible. Christ is not only available but accessible. He is the accessible Christ. The sinner has ready access to Him. The saving word is nigh to the sinner's mouth for confession and to the sinner's heart for belief as it is declared through the preaching of Sovereign Grace. By the preaching of the Inspired Word the Incarnate Word draws near and goes with us. Christ is gloriously accessible.

The words which Moses spake in Deuteronomy 30:11-14 were prophetic of the accessibility of Christ:

"For this commandment which I command thee this day, it is not hidden from thee, neither is it far off. It is not in heaven, that thou shouldst say, Who shall go up for us to heaven, and bring it unto us, that we may hear it, and do it? Neither is it beyond the sea, that thou shouldest say, Who shall go over the sea for us, and bring it unto us, that we may hear it, and do it? But the word is very nigh unto thee, in thy mouth, and in thy heart, that thou mayest do it".

Every time, the gospel preacher can say to his hearers, as Christ said to His, "notwithstanding, be ye sure of this, the Kingdom of God is come unto you" (Luke 10:11).

3.   THE PROMISE OF THE PREACHING, vs. 9-13

The preaching conveys to men the great and glorious promise of the true Gospel. In each of these verses we have a brilliant facet of the gospel diadem of promise.

(a) *The Steps of the Promise*

"That if thou shalt confess with thy mouth the Lord Jesus, and shalt believe in thine heart that God hath raised Him from the dead, thou shalt be saved", v. 9. There are two steps in the promise, confession with the mouth and belief with the heart. Both the confession which is outward and manward, and the belief which is inward and Godward are related to the Person and the work of Christ. For Christ is the gospel and the gospel is Christ. They are also inseparably linked together. The confession is a mouth confession concerning the Lordship of Christ, "if thou shalt confess with thy mouth the Lord Jesus or Jesus is Lord". This involves the renunciation of the lordship of Satan, self and sin and the taking of the oath of allegiance to Christ. Only by the power of the Holy Spirit can this be accomplished, "no man can say that Jesus is the Lord but by the Holy Ghost" (I Cor. 12:3).

The belief is a heart belief concerning the Resurrection of the Lord Jesus by God from among the dead. The resurrection is the climax and coronation of the whole life and death of the Lord Jesus. It is the mighty culmination of the finished work of redemption, the heavenly approbation or approval that Christ had completed the work which God had given Him to do.

> *"The Lord is risen indeed,*
> *Now is His Work performed;*
> *Now is the mighty captive freed,*
> *And death's strong castle stormed."*

This heart belief is saving faith, and Christ is exalted to give it to His people (Acts 5:31).

(b) *The Salvation of the Promise*

"For with the heart man believeth unto righteousness: and with the mouth confession is made unto salvation", v. 10.

The promise is the promise of salvation. This salvation is the result of justifying righteousness, "for with the heart man believeth unto righteousness". Christ has accomplished this justifying righteousness for all who believe. The salvation promised is a salvation based on the satisfying of every claim of the inflexible law and the putting away of sin by the full payment of the penalty incurred.

> *"The just for the unjust,*
> *Has died on the tree;*
> *That's my way to God,*
> *And it's God's way to me."*

With the mouth confession is made unto this salvation based upon peace with God through our Lord Jesus Christ.

(c) *The Security of the Promise*

"For the scripture saith, Whosoever believeth on Him shall not be ashamed", v. 11.

The security of the promise is the Word of God. The text is a quotation from Isaiah 28:16. See also Romans 9:33. Now the Lord Jesus Christ declared that "the scripture cannot be broken" (John 10:35), so the promise of scripture is impregnable. No potency can disintegrate this rock.

(d) *The Source of the Promise*

"For there is no difference between the Jew and the Greek; for the same Lord over all is rich unto all that call upon Him," v. 12.

The source is inexhaustible. It is God who is rich. This richness is dispensed without distinction, "for there is no difference (lit. "no distinction") between the Jew and the Greek".

Elsewhere in the epistle we have revealed wherein God is rich toward sinners. In chapter two, verse four, we are told of "the riches of His goodness and forbearance and long-suffering", In chapter nine, verse twenty-three, we are told of "the riches of His Glory", while chapter eleven, verse thirty-three, tells of "the riches both of the wisdom and knowledge of God". So God is rich toward us in goodness, forbearance, long-suffering, glory, wisdom and knowledge. What inexhaustible riches! the inexhaustible source of the inexhaustible salvation.

(e) *The Simplicity of the Promise*

"For whosoever shall call upon the name of the Lord shall be saved", v. 13.

(1)	The broadest possible invitation.	"Whosoever" lit. "everyone whoever".
(2)	The easiest possible condition.	"shall call" lit. "cry".
(3)	The simplest possible supplication.	"on the name of the Lord".
(4)	The greatest possible salvation.	"shall be saved".

4. THE PLACE OF THE PREACHING, vs. 14-17

The preacher has a very important place in the gospel economy. Modern twentieth century Christianity makes little of the preacher. Primitive first century Christianity makes much of the preacher. Preaching is God's method of winning souls. The preacher's place of importance is set forth in these verses in four ways.

(a) *The Preacher and His Congregation*
"How then shall they call on Him in whom they have not believed? and how shall they believe in Him of whom they have not heard? and how shall they hear without a preacher?" v. 14.

The place of the preacher, when viewed from the aspect of his congregation, is most important. Without the preacher they will most surely perish. He is essential to their hearing; hearing is essential to their believing; believing is essential to their calling; and calling is essential to their salvation, see verse 13.

(1) *Hearing*
In order to be saved, the Word of God must be heard. This is of vital importance for how shall they hear without a preacher? Paul lays great stress in this chapter upon the spoken word, the word preached. "For "Word" he uses a term which means "the spoken word". In verse eight he speaks of "the word (the spoken word) is nigh thee". Further in the same verse he says "the word (spoken word) of faith, which we preach". In verse seventeen he uses the same term again, "hearing by the word (spoken word) of God". In verse eighteen he uses it yet again, "their words (spoken words) unto the ends of the earth". In order to provide hearing of the word the preacher is an absolute necessity. He is the channel of the Word of God. By him it becomes the spoken word.

(2) *Believing*
The hearing begets the believing. This we shall consider further in verse seventeen.

(3) *Calling*
The calling results from the believing. Life itself begotten, begets the cry. In order to provide all three the preaching is a divinely ordained necessity.

(b) *The Preacher and His Commission*
"And how shall they preach, except they be sent? as it is written, How beautiful are the feet of them that preach the gospel of peace, and bring glad tidings of good things!" v. 15.

The preacher must be commissioned by the Lord. He himself is unimportant but his importance is attached to his Divine appointment. In ecclesiastical circles today the emphasis is usually on "the call of the people". So and so "has received a call" is frequently heard in church business gatherings. The New Testament preachers were sent. There is a great difference between a sent preacher and a called parson. Called parsons win silver, but the sent preacher wins souls. The merely called parson is despised but the sent preacher is respected. His place is both honourable and beautiful. Paul uses two Old Testament scriptures to prove this, see Isaiah 52:7 and Nahum 1:15.

(c) *The Preacher and his Concern*

"But they have not all obeyed the gospel. For Esaias saith, Lord, who hath believed our report?" v. 16. The disobedience of souls weighs heavily upon the preacher. He is concerned and cries out like Isaiah in both amazement and consternation, "Who hath believed our report?" The preacher is one of the Lord's remembrances and will "give him no rest, till He establish, and till he make Jerusalem a praise in the earth", see Isaiah 62:7.

Such is the place of the preacher.

(d) *The Preacher and His Conclusion*

"So then faith cometh by hearing, and hearing by the word of God", v. 17.

The conclusion of the preacher discovers to himself his own awful responsibility. Faith is begotten in his hearers by the Word of God, spoken through his lips. The spoken word is the seed which brings forth eternal life. The sower soweth the seed and the seed is the word of God (Luke 8:11). Note carefully in the interpretation of the parable the word had to be heard. "Those by the wayside are they that *hear*" (Luke 8:12). "They on the rocks are they, which, when they *hear*" (Luke 8:13). "And that which fell among the thorns are they, which, when they have *heard*" (Luke 8:14).

"That on good ground are they, having *heard* the word" (Luke 8:15).

Peter writes, "Being born again, not of corruptible seed, but of incorruptible, by the word of God, which liveth and abideth forever. For all flesh is as grass, and all the glory of man as the flower of grass. The grass withereth, and the flower thereof falleth away; but the word of the Lord endureth for ever. And this is the word which by the gospel is preached unto you" (I Pet. 1:23-25). Notice it is again on the Word *preached* that the emphasis is laid. This is the Divine method. May God bless every faithful preacher of His Word!

5.   **THE PARADOX OF THE PREACHING**
      "But I say, have they not heard? Yes verily, their sound went into
      all the earth, and their words unto the ends of the world. But I say,
      Did not Israel know? First Moses saith, I will provoke you to
      jealousy by them that are no people and by a foolish nation I will
      anger you. But Esaias is very bold, and saith, I was found of them
      that sought me not; I was made manifest unto them that asked not
      after me. But to Israel He saith, All day long I have stretched forth
      my hands unto a disobedient and gainsaying people", vs. 18-21.

      Yes, Paul argues that the spoken word has sounded out to the ends of the
earth and there is therefore no excuse for Israel who were the first to receive the
message. It would be thought that those first to hear would have been first to
believe. This however is not so. Those who are believers are the most unlikely,
humanly speaking. God is found of those who sought him not. The foolish nation
enters in while the nation of knowledge holds back. Those who, humanly
speaking, ought to be saved remain disobedient and gainsaying. This is the
paradox of preaching.
      Nevertheless, the foundation of God standeth sure and His never failing
purpose is unfolded in the next chapter.

[This section completed on the seventy-fifth day of imprisonment:
Monday, 3rd October, 1966]

11 The purpose of
Sovereign Grace

IN CHAPTER NINE we have studied the Principle of Sovereign Grace, and in chapter ten the Preaching of Sovereign Grace. Now in chapter eleven we come to a consideration of the Purpose of Sovereign Grace.

The chapter brings before us five aspects of the Purpose of Sovereign Grace.

1.   THE PURPOSE OF GRACE ESTABLISHED BY ELECTION
"I say then, Hath God cast away his people? God forbid. For I am also an Israelite, of the seed of Abraham, of the tribe of Benjamin. God hath not cast away his people which He foreknew. Wot ye not what the scripture saith of Elias? how he maketh intercession to God against Israel, saying, Lord they have killed thy prophets, and digged down thine altars; and I am left alone, and they seek my life. But what saith the answer of God unto him? I have reserved to myself seven thousand men, who have not bowed the knee to the image of Baal. Even so then at this present time also there is a remnant according to the election of grace. And if by grace, then it is no more of works: otherwise grace is no more grace. But if it be of works, then is it no more grace; otherwise work is no more work", vs. 1-6.

Looking over the world and knowing something of the promises of God to Israel and Paul's previous teaching of the immortality of those very promises the objection may well be made and the question asked, "Hath God cast away his people?"

Paul answers this objection in a twofold manner, by an appeal to himself and by an appeal to Holy Scripture. "Look at me" he says, "I am proof positive that God hath not cast away His people whom He foreknew". Every converted Jew is a living testimony to this insurmountable fact. Secondly, Paul appeals to the Holy Scripture. He recalls the case of Elijah and the apostasy of Israel under Baal. He describes the intercession of the man of God. "Lord, they have killed Thy prophets, and digged down Thine altars; and I am left alone, and they seek my life", v. 3. He then reminds us of the Lord's answer concerning the reservation of seven thousand who have not bowed the knee to the image of Baal.

Having laid the foundation with this scriptural fact he then erects the grand conclusion of verse 5, "E'en so then at this present time also there is a remnant according to the election of grace". The purpose of God is established by the election. This purpose is entirely of grace. Works to which a blinded Israel clung, wield no authority here. Paul concludes this section with the enunciation of the great definition and grand conclusion of verse six. "And if by grace, then it is no more of works; otherwise grace is no more grace. But if it be of works, then it is no more grace. Otherwise work is no more work."

2.   **THE PURPOSE OF GRACE EXPLAINED BY PROPHECY**
"What then? Israel hath not obtained that which he seeketh for; but the election hath obtained it, and the rest were blinded. (According as it is written, God hath given them the spirit of slumber, eyes that they should not see, and ears that they should not hear;) unto this day. And David saith, Let their table be made a snare, and a trap, and a stumblingblock, and a recompense unto them: let their eyes be darkened, that they may not see, and bow down their back alway. I say then, Have they stumbled that they should fall? God forbid; but rather through their fall, salvation is come unto the Gentiles, for to provoke them to jealousy. Now if the fall of them be the riches of the world, and the diminishing of them the riches of the Gentiles; how much more their fulness?" vs. 7-12.

Though Israel as a nation has not obtained salvation, "that which he seeketh for", yet the remnant according to the election of grace has obtained it, v. 7. The rest have been left in the blindness of their ignorance through gainsaying and disobedience (Rom. 10:21).

Prophecy explains this blindness as mysteriously working out the purpose of Grace.

Two quotations are given. The first in verse eight is from Isaiah. Two passages are, I believe, in the apostle's mind, Isaiah 6:9 and 10 and Isaiah 29:10. The second quotation in verses nine and ten is from Psalm 69:22, 23. These prophetic scriptures are worthy of close attention. The passages from Isaiah deal with Israel's rejection of the Divine message and the resulting blindness of heart of the nation. The passage from the Psalms deals with the rejection of the Divine Messiah and the resulting curse upon the people. The previous verse to the two quoted is verse 21 and it reads, "They gave me also gall for my meat; and in my thirst they gave me vinegar to drink". The connection with Christ is thus very evident.

Prophecy, then, explains the purpose of grace showing how Israel fell by rejecting the Divine Messenger and His message. In their fall, however, they are prepared for an even greater exaltation than they had before their fall. They are not fallen forever. "Have they stumbled that they should fall (i.e. forever)? God forbid", v. 11. Rather by their fall the Gentiles received the Messiah which they rejected and the saving message which they refused. Seeing the purpose of Grace so wonderfully explained by prophecy, Paul can do no other but ask the question of verse 12, "Now if the fall of them be the riches of the world, and the diminishing of them (their reduction to a remnant) the riches of the Gentiles; how much more their fulness?"

3.   **THE PURPOSE OF GRACE EXPOUNDED BY ANALOGY**
"For I speak to you Gentiles, inasmuch as I am the apostle of the Gentiles, I magnify mine office; if by any means I may provoke to emulation them which are my flesh, and might save some of them, For if the casting away of them be the reconciling of the world, what shall the receiving of them be, but life from the dead? For if the first fruit be holy, the lump is also holy; and if the root be holy, so are the branches. And if some of the branches be broken off, and thou, being a wild olive tree, were graffed in among them, and with them partaketh of the root and fatness of the olive tree; boast not against the branches. But if thou boast, thou bearest not the root, but the root thee. Thou wilt say then, The branches were broken off, that I might be graffed in. Well; because of unbelief they were

broken off, and thou standest by faith. Be not highminded, but fear; For if God spared not the natural branches, take heed lest he also spare not thee. Behold therefore the goodness and severity of God; on them which fell, severity; but towards thee, goodness, if thou continue in His goodness; otherwise thou also shalt be cut off. And they also, if they abide not still in unbelief, shall be graffed in: for God is able to graff them in again. For if thou were cut out of the olive tree which is wild by nature, and wert graffed contrary to nature into a good olive tree; how much more shall these, which be the natural branches, be graffed into their own olive tree?" vs. 13-25.

The purpose of grace is clearly stated in verse 15: "For if the casting away of them be the reconciling of the world, what shall the receiving of them be, but life from the dead?" There is nothing ambiguous about this statement. Its teaching is plain. Israel's receiving again is just as certain as her casting away has been. In that casting away there has been reconciliation (the reconciling of the world) and in the receiving of them there shall be resurrection (life from the dead).

The following verses expound this glorious purpose under the analogy of the good olive tree. The good olive tree represents the Israel of God with its root in divine election and its fatness in Divine salvation. Now certain branches were broken off. This represents Israel at the time of their national rejection of the Messiah. "He came unto His own, and His own received Him not" (John 1:11). "Because of unbelief they were broken off", v. 20. The wild olive tree is the Gentiles. The branches cut off from the wild olive tree (v. 24) and graffed into the good olive tree are those Gentiles who believed. By grafting they partook of the root and fatness of the good olive. The believing Gentiles partake of the root of Divine election and the fruit of Divine salvation. They dare not boast, however, for they bear not the root but the root bears them (v. 18). The "sparing not" of unbelieving Israel is a solemn warning to them lest they also through unbelief be broken off, v. 21.

The good olive tree with the natural branches broken off and branches of the wild olive grafted in is a manifested testimony to the goodness and severity of God, v. 22.

That is not the end of the analogy. There is still hope for Israel if they abide not still in unbelief, v. 23. The hand that broke them off can graft them in again. This is undoubtedly the purpose of grace and Paul closes the section with the great question of verse 24. "For if thou wert cut out of the olive tree which is wild by nature, and wert graffed contrary to nature into a good olive tree; how much more shall these, which be the natural branches, be graffed into their own olive tree?"

4.   THE PURPOSE OF GRACE EXPRESSED IN SCRIPTURE

"For I would not, brethren, that ye should be ignorant of tis mystery, lest ye should be wise in our own conceits; that blindness in part is happened to Israel, until the fulness of the Gentiles be come in. And so all Israel shall be saved; as it is written, There shall come out of Sion the Deliverer, and shall turn away ungodliness from Jacob: for this is my covenant unto them, when I shall take away their sins. As concerning the gospel, they are enemies for your sakes; but as touching the election, they are beloved for the fathers' sakes. For the gifts and calling of God are without repentance. For as ye in times past have not believed God, yet have now obtained mercy through their unbelief: Even so have these also now not believed, that through your mercy they also may obtain mercy. For God hath concluded them all in unbelief, that He might have mercy upon all," vs. 25-32.

Scripture is a revelation of God's mysteries. Paul uses the word "mystery" many times in his epistles.

The word he uses for mystery means "what is known to the initiated". It is the revealed mystery known to the initiated as opposed to the hidden unknown mystery. Now the mystery of the purpose of grace concerning Israel is not hidden but made known to those instructed in the Scripture. The believing Gentile is not to be wise in his own conceits, v. 25. By all devotees of all schools of prophecy this word should be carefully heeded. Submission to the word of God is the true wisdom. Blindness (lit. "hardness") has happened in part unto Israel, v. 25. It is only in part, however, for the remnant according to the election of grace are saved through faith by grace. Note, the termination of the time of this prevailing unbelief of Israel, in the expression, "until the fulness of the Gentiles be come in", v. 25. Israel is not to be hardened forever. As far as the gospel now preached amongst the Gentiles is concerned, unbelieving Israel is the enemy. This enmity resulting from their casting away has been ordained by God for the Gentiles' sake, v. 28. In this period of Israel's enmity the Gentiles have heard the gospel and their fulness is being ushered in. The Gentiles must however see beyond Israel's enmity and realise that , "as touching the election (i.e. the full purpose of grace, in God receiving Israel again, v. 15), they are beloved for the fathers' sake", v. 28. The fathers I take to mean their national or founding fathers, Abraham, Isaac and Jacob. In this it must ever be remembered that the gifts and calling of God are without repentance, v. 29. God's purpose will be fulfilled and God's promise will be honoured. Scripture expresses this purpose of Grace thus:

"And so all Israel shall be saved; as it is written. There shall come out of Sion the Deliverer, and shall turn away ungodliness from Jacob: For this is my covenant unto them, when I shall take away their sins", vs. 26, 27.

The expression "all Israel" is limited to Israel at the particular time of their receiving again by God when the fulness of the Gentiles is come. It is also qualified by the expression of verse 23 "if they abide not still in unbelief". Faith in Christ grafted the branches of the wild olive into the good olive and like precious faith in Christ will graft in the broken-off branches into heir own natural root. "For as ye in times past have not believed God, yet have now obtained mercy through their unbelief; even so have these also now not believed, that through your mercy they also may obtain mercy", vs. 30, 31.

Christ is the executor of this great eternal design and His covenant will He not break, nor alter the thing that has gone out of His mouth. Isaac, though he long tarried, came forth at last from the womb of Sarah and this Isaac of covenant promise though it has long tarried, shall also come forth at last from the womb of God's great eternal purpose. Then shall Israel arise and shine for her light will have come and the glory of God will have risen upon her (Isa. 59:20, 21; 60:1). (*Jews and Gentiles by the same method.*) The last verse of this section, v. 32, declares how God saves both.

5.   THE PURPOSE OF GRACE EXTOLLED IN DOXOLOGY, vs. 33-36

Paul can no longer contain himself so he burst out into grand doxology extolling the purpose of grace. The doxology has three parts.

(a) *Extolling the Might of God's Purpose*

"O the depth of the riches both of the wisdom and knowledge of God! How unsearchable are His judgments, and His ways past finding out! For who hath known the mind of the Lord? or who hath been His counsellor?" vs. 33, 34.

Here we have:

(1) Depths which cannot be fathomed.

(2) Judgments which cannot be searched.

(3) Ways which cannot be found.

(4) A Mind which cannot be known.

(5) Counsel which cannot be assisted.

(b) *Extolling the Mysteries of God's Purpose*

"Or who hath first given to Him, and it shall be recompensed unto him again?" v. 35.

(c) *Extolling the Majesty of God's Purpose*

"For of Him, and through Him, and to Him, are all things: to whom be glory forever". Amen

[Finished this chapter on the seventy-seventh day of imprisonment, Wednesday, 5th October, 1966]

12 **Our individual**
responsibility

IN CHAPTER TWELVE we enter into the practical section of the epistle. Chapters 1-11 are doctrinal, what we ought to believe; chapters 12-15 are practical, what we ought to do, chapter 16 is the postscript containing personal greetings by Paul to various members of the church. The two parts doctrinal and practical are common to all Paul's epistles. This is the rule of his epistology. Both parts conclude with benediction or doxology and Amen, as also do the postscripts. Compare Romans 11:36; 15:33 and 16:27.

In chapters 12-15 are set forth our responsibilities as believers:

Chapter 12 - Our Individual Responsibility.

Chapter 13 - Our Social Responsibility.

Chapter 14 - Our Fraternal Responsibility.

Chapter 15 - Our Universal Responsibility.

1.   OUR INDIVIDUAL RESPONSIBILITY - SPIRITUALLY, vs. 1-3

(a) *Towards God*

"I beseech you therefore, brethren, by the mercies of God, that ye present your bodies a living sacrifice, holy, acceptable unto God, which is your reasonable service", v. 1.

This verse reads literally, "I exhort you therefore brethren by the compassion of God to present your bodies a living sacrifice, holy, well pleasing to God, your intelligent service."

Here we have

(1) *The Dynamic Exhortation*

"I exhort you therefore brethren by the compassion of God".

Paul exhorts by the compassion of God. The depths of these compassions he has expounded in the preceding doctrinal section of the epistle. What depths of compassion are discovered in the statement of chapter five, verse eight, "But God commendeth His love toward us, in that, while we were yet sinners, Christ died for us!"

(2) *The Demanded Presentation*

"to present your bodies a living sacrifice, holy, well pleasing to God".

Our bodies are to be finally redeemed. This is the full manifestation of our adoption as sons (Romans 8:23). The presentation of these bodies now to God as a living sacrifice on the altar is our spiritual responsibility. This presentation is holy, well pleasing to God because of the operation of the sacred principle that the altar sanctifieth the gift (Matt. 23:19).

(3) *The Decisive Argumentation*

"your intelligent service".

This presentation demanded is intelligent and responsible. If, in the future, God is going to redeem this body for all eternity on the basis of the giving of His Son's precious body on the tree, is it not reasonable that I should right now give my body to Him for His own use and service in time? "Here, Lord, I give myself away, 'tis all that I can do".

(b) *Towards the World*

"And be not conformed to this world: but be transformed by the renewing of your mind, that ye may prove what is that good, and acceptable, and perfect will of God", v. 2.

Every believer is to be a nonconformist, a nonconformist to this present evil age. (The word translated "world" means "age".) Conformity to the age is the curse of the church of our day. RB Jones, the great revival preacher of Wales, once called the devil "the ape of God", that is, the devil apes or tries to make himself like God.

How tragic when Christians ape the worldlings preferring the muck-rake to the golden crown.

Instead of conformity to the god of this age we are called to a blessed uniformity with the God of all ages. O the sweetness of the uniformity of His blessed will! Herein is satisfaction of soul for it is good and acceptable (lit. "well pleasing") and perfect or complete. This comes by the transformation wrought when the mind is renewed by the Holy Ghost. Our spiritual responsibility is not to conform but to be transformed.

(c) *Towards self*

"For I say, through the grace given unto me, to every man that is among you, not to think of himself more highly than he ought to think; but to think soberly, according as God has dealt to every man the measure of faith", v. 3.

Our spiritual responsibility as regards ourselves is for constant humility. Scriptural sobriety is a spur to this humility. We must ever seek to heed the word of the ancient prophet:

"He hath shewed thee, O man, what is good; and what doth the Lord require of thee, but to do justly, and to love mercy, and walk to humbly with thy God?" (Mic. 6:8).

2. OUR INDIVIDUAL RESPONSIBILITY - ECCLESIASTICALLY

"For as we have many members in one body, and all members have not the same office: so we, being many, are one body in Christ, and everyone members one of another. Having then gifts differing according to the grace that is given to us, whether prophecy, let us prophesy according to the proportion of faith; or ministry, let us wait on our ministering; or he that teacheth, on teaching, or he that exhorteth, on exhortation; he that giveth, let him do it with simplicity; he that ruleth, with diligence; he that sheweth mercy, with cheerfulness." vs. 4-8.

These verses deal with our personal ecclesiastical responsibility or our individual responsibility in the church. We are all members of Christ's one body but we have not all the same office. There is a blessed unity in membership but a bountiful diversity in office. It is our individual responsibility in the church to exercise our gift and magnify our office. Paul lists seven offices (seven is one of the perfect numbers, in scripture); the office of prophet, i.e. preacher or teller-forth;

minister; teacher; exhorter; giver; ruler and dispenser, and exhorts those specially gifted to occupy these several offices to fulfil in God's will their respective duties. He stresses our individual responsibility in the church.

3.   OUR INDIVIDUAL RESPONSIBILITY - CHARITABLY, vs. 9-21

The Christian is not under the law as a way to life but the Christian is under the law as a rule of life. Now love is the fulfilling of the law and this is our individual responsibility (Rom. 13:10).

"Let love be without dissimulation", v. 9.

Love must be pure, not feigned nor hypocritical. The love which the ecumenists bleat about is full of dissimulation. They breathe charity to the antichrist and his worshippers and hatred to the true Christ and His worshippers.

"Abhor that which is evil; cleave to that which is good".

Love *negatively*, repudiates evil (lit. "shrinks away from"), separates from evil and *positively* cleaves, embraces, that which is good. The so-called love which cleaves to evil, evil teachers, evil systems, evil confederations, evil doctrines and evil associations, is a bastard charity, the offspring of hell itself. "Be kindly affectionate one to another with brotherly love; in honour preferring one another", v. 10.

Love's fraternity is characterised by humility.

"Not slothful in business; fervent in spirit; serving the Lord", v. 11.

Love is not a sleepy sloth but a serving slave.

"Rejoicing in hope; patient in tribulation; continuing instant in prayer", v. 12.

Love leads in praise, patience and prayer.

"Distributing to the necessity of saints; given to hospitality", v. 13.

Love distributes with a full hand and lays a rich table.

"Bless them which persecute you; bless, and curse not", v. 14.

Love's lips are pure and bless the persecutor and curse not.

"Rejoice with them that do rejoice, and weep with them that weep", v. 15.

Love is at home both in the house of mourning and the house of merriment.

"Be of the same mind one toward another. Mind not high things, but condescend to men of low estate. Be not wise in your own conceits", v. 16. Love is the great unifier and reconciler and she is always clad in the garments of humility and service.

"Recompense to no man evil for evil", v. 17.

Love pays all her debts in the same coin of affection.

"Provide things honest in the sight of all men", v. 17.

Love is strictly honest in business.

"If it be possible, as much as lieth in you, live peaceably with all men", v. 18.

Love seeks peace but never at the price of truth.

"Dearly beloved, avenge not yourselves, but rather give place unto wrath; for it is written, Vengeance is mine; I will repay, saith the Lord", v. 19.

Love avenges not but leaves vengeance to the Lord.

"Therefore if thine enemy hunger, feed him; if he thirst, give him drink; for in so doing thou shalt heap coals of fire on his head", v. 20.

Love disarms the enemy with generosity.

"Be not overcome of evil, but overcome evil with good", v. 21.

Love wins the overcomer's crown at last.

[This chapter completed on the seventy-eighth day of imprisonment: Thursday, 6th October, 1966]

13 Our social *responsibility*

EVERY CHRISTIAN HAS a responsibility in and towards the society in which God in providence has placed him. He has a vital contribution to make towards its prosperity and well-being. The Christian's separation must never be an isolation like the perversity of monasticism. Alas, monasticism is not limited to Romanism! The Christians are the salt of the earth and have a vital responsibility to act as a strong preservative in the society in which they are placed. Those Christians who refuse to fulfil their social responsibilities are acting contrary to the plain teaching of scripture.

This chapter sets forth our responsibilities towards the Magistrates, the Mandates and the Members of our society.

1.   **OUR RESPONSIBILITY TOWARDS THE MAGISTRATES OF SOCIETY, vs. 1-5**
      "Let every soul be subject unto the higher powers. For there is no power but of God: the powers that be are ordained of God. Whosoever therefore resisteth the power, resisteth the ordinance of God: and they that resist shall receive to themselves damnation. For rulers are not a terror to good works, but to the evil. Wilt thou then not be afraid of the power? do that which is good, and thou

shalt have praise of the same. For he is the minister of God to thee for good. But if thou do that which is evil, be afraid; for he beareth not the sword in vain: for he is the minister of God, a revenger to execute wrath upon him that doeth evil. Wherefore ye must needs be subject, not only for wrath, but also for conscience sake."

It must be said clearly at the outset that these verses do not apply to laws contrary to the law of God. Robert Haldane said once, preaching from the first verse. "There is but one exception and that is, when anything is required contrary to the law of God". For this we have the plainest apostolic example and teaching, "Then Peter and the other apostles answered and said, We ought to obey God rather than men" (Acts 5:29).

Certain people who wish to bolster up a rotten government and the persecuting laws of the same, condemn the resistance of the martyrs, reformers, confessors, non-conformists, puritans and covenanters to the evil laws and governments of their day, and to all who would follow in their train in this our own generation. These misguided and Biblically untaught folks take the line of least resistance to evil and seek scripturally to establish their false position. This they accomplish by wresting this and other scriptures to their own destruction. A careful study of these verses refutes their futile arguments for base compromise and baser betrayal of the faith of Christ. It is clear from these verses that God has ordained and delegated powers to various departments of society. For example, the father is the divinely ordained power in the family, the basic unit of society. This does not mean that God ordains and approves every wicked, immoral, murderous brute of a father who is a tyrant in his home. The office of father, the power of the father, is divinely ordained but the abuse of the office is not divinely ordained. The ordination has to do with the office and not with the character of the occupant of that office. In society the authorities are ordained of God in regard to their office or power but not in regard to their characters. The chief magistrate is divinely ordained, the office is sacred, but a Hitler who usurps and abuses the office is not divinely ordained neither are the laws of such a tyrant to be obeyed when they oppose the law of God. Paul speaks clearly on the nature of the laws he has in mind when he says, "For rulers are not a terror to good works, but to the evil. Wilt thou then not be afraid of the power? Do that which is good, and thou shalt have praise of the same", v. 3.

Here we have the magistrate as a minister of God magnifying his divinely ordained office by praising that which is good and by executing wrath on that which is evil.

There is a vast difference between this kind of magistrate and those who readily accept the testimony of perjured law men, who have men's persons in admiration because of advantage and who condemn faithful preachers to unjust imprisonment on blatantly false evidence concocted by the scheming of corrupted and perverted politicians. Such magistrates, who have persecuted the church in all ages, receive no praise from God but rather His curse, see Micah 3:9-12 and 7:3, 4. Only uninstructed misguided Christians would condone, defend and submit to such malpractices.

2.   **OUR RESPONSIBILITY TOWARDS THE MANDATES OF SOCIETY, vs. 6-8**
   "For this cause pay ye tribute also; for they are God's ministers, attending continually upon this very thing. Render therefore to all their dues; tribute to whom tribute is due; custom to whom custom; fear to whom fear; honour to whom honour. Owe no man anything, but to love one another, for he that loveth another hath fulfilled the law."

The lawful mandate of society must be submitted to by the Christian. The demands of the government upon our money must be instantly obeyed. We must in obedience to the command of our Lord Jesus Christ "Render to Caesar the things that are Caesar's" (Mark 12:17). A Christian is under solemn divine obligation to pay lawful rates and taxes, tributes and customs, v. 7.

A Christian must also give due and proper respect to those above him in society. The motive for this is not base servility but Divine charity as set forth in verse 8.

3.   **OUR RESPONSIBILITY TOWARDS THE MEMBERS OF SOCIETY, vs. 9, 10.**
   "For this, Thou shalt not commit adultery, Thou shalt not kill, Thou shalt not steal, Thou shalt not bear false witness, Thou shalt not covet; and if there be any other commandment, it is briefly comprehended in this saying, namely, Thou shalt love thy neighbour as thyself. Love worketh no ill to his neighbour; therefore love is the fulfilling of the law."

Here we have the law as the Christian's rule of life. It is our responsibility to help and not to harm every member of society. We are not to commit adultery for that would harm our neighbour's wife or husband; we are not to kill as that would harm our neighbour's life; we are not to bear false witness as that would harm our neighbour's character and we are not to covet as that would harm our neighbour's security. We are to love our neighbours as ourselves for love is the fulfilling of the law, v. 10.

An Exhortation, vs. 11-14

"And that, knowing the time, that now it is high time to wake out of sleep; for now is our salvation nearer than when we believed. The night is far spent, the day is at hand; let us therefore cast off the works of darkness, and let us put on the armour of light. Let us walk honestly, as in the day; not in rioting and drunkenness, not in chambering and wantonness, not in strife and envying. But put ye on the Lord Jesus Christ and make not provision for the flesh, to fulfil the lusts thereof," vs. 11-14.

The chapter ends with a solemn exhortation. The man right within, will be the man right without. The day of God's judgment approaches and we must live ever in its all-revealing light, vs. 11, 12.

Our walk should not be characterised by any of these six things (six is the number of man and flesh) rioting and drunkenness, chambering and wantonness and strife and envying, v. 13. This we can achieve as we put on the Lord Jesus Christ and "make not provision for the flesh, to fulfil the lusts thereof", v. 14.

[This chapter completed on Friday, 7th October, 1966, seventy-ninth day of imprisonment]

14 Our fraternal *responsibility*

THIS CHAPTER EXPOUNDS our fraternal responsibility - the responsibility to our brethren. It sets forth some practices of brethren and then gives some guiding principles which we must follow in order to discharge our fraternal responsibilities. The theme of the chapter runs over into chapter fifteen concluding at verse seven. So we must take these seven verses of chapter fifteen along with chapter fourteen.

1. THE PRACTICES OF THE BRETHREN
"Him that is weak in the faith receive ye, but not to doubtful disputations" (14:1).
"Wherefore receive ye one another as Christ also received us to the glory of God" (15:7).

The first and last verses of this section of the epistle on our fraternal responsibility should be compared. The commands in both are similar, the weaker brother is not to be excommunicated but rather he is to be received. We must of course make sure he is in reality a brother and not a hypocrite feigning to be a weaker brother for his own advantage. Hence we have the warning in chapter fourteen verse one, "but not to doubtful disputations", and the qualification in chapter fifteen verse seven, "as Christ also received us", the "us" referring both to the weak and strong in faith.

(a) Practices of Diet

"For one believeth that he may eat all things; another, who is weak, eateth herbs. Let not him that eateth despise him that eateth not; and let not him which eateth not judge him that eateth: for God hath received him" vs. 2,3.

The weaker brother is not strong enough to exercise his full liberty in Christ. The one strong in faith eats all things, even the meat which in the pagan cattle mart had been dedicated to idols. In the first epistle to the Corinthians, Paul takes up this subject.

"As concerning therefore the eating of those things that are offered in sacrifice unto idols, we know that an idol is nothing in the world, and that there is none other God but one. For though there be that are called gods, whether in heaven or in earth (as there be gods many, and lords many) but to us there is but one God, the Father, of whom are all things, and we in Him; and one Lord Jesus Christ, by whom are all things, and we by Him. Howbeit there is not in every man that knowledge: for some with conscience of the idol unto this hour eat it as a thing offered unto an idol; and their conscience being weak is defiled. But meat commendeth us not unto God: for neither if we eat are we the better; neither if we eat not, are we the worse. But take heed lest by any means this liberty of yours become a stumbling block to them that are weak" (1 Cor. 8:4-9).

The weaker brother deplores the eating of meats and goes back to the divinely prescribed diet of innocent Adam and the natural creation yet unfallen.

"And God said, Behold, I have given you every herb bearing seed, which is upon the face of all the earth, and every tree, in which is the fruit of a tree yielding seed; to you it shall be for meat. And to every beast of the earth, and to every fowl of the air, and everything that creepeth on the earth, wherein there is life, I have given every green herb for meat: and it was so" (Gen. 1:29,30).

The brethren strong in faith were in grave danger of despising the weaker brethren for their abstention from meat. Yes, and the weaker brethren were also in grave danger of condemning the strong brethren for their partaking of meat. Hence the statement of Paul rebuking both parties "God hath received him " (i.e. both strong and weak).

(b) Practices of Days

"One man esteemeth one day above another; another esteemeth every day alike. Let every man be fully persuaded in his own mind. He that regardeth the day, regardeth it unto the Lord; and he that regardeth not the day, to the Lord he doth not regard it. He that eateth, eateth to the Lord, for he giveth God thanks; and he that eateth not to the Lord he eateth not and giveth God thanks" vs 5-6. The transition from the old to the new, from law to grace, from the Mosaic economy to the Christian, brought various views in regard to feast days and the necessity of observing the same. The Lord's Day is not in question here for its keeping was clearly manifested in apostolic practice.

For example we read in Acts 20:7: "And upon the first day of the week, when the disciples came together to break bread, Paul preached unto them".

Further, we have the command, "Upon the first day of the week let everyone of you lay by him in store, as God hath prospered him, that there be no gatherings when I come" (I Cor. 16:2).

Paul had no doubt in mind the other days also called sabbaths or rest days. These troubled those weak in faith and they esteemed them above other days. The strong in faith enjoying the full liberty in Christ looked upon these all as alike. Paul points out that if a day is kept, as long as it is kept unto the Lord it is quite in order. The brother, however, who does not keep the day because of a clearer knowledge of God's Word is also in order. The parallel of this issue concerning days is that concerning diets and a similar apostolic finding in both cases is here declared. Colossians 2:16 and 17 should be noted in this connection: "Let no man judge therefore you in meat, or in drink, or in respect of an holy day (feast day) or of the new moon, or of the sabbath days (weeks) which are a shadow of things to come; but the body is of Christ."

The word holy day is feast day. In the phrase "of the sabbath days", the word "days" is in italics, which means that it is not in the original. "Sabbath" is in the plural, "sabbaths" and can be translated "weeks". The phrase then reads, "of weeks", meaning Passover weeks and the other weeks of Jewish feasts which were mainly made up of days called sabbaths or rest days.

(c) The Practices of Denunciation

"Who art thou that judgest another man's servant? to his own master he standeth or falleth. Yea, he shall be holden up; for God is able to make him stand" v.4.

"But why dost thou judge thy brother? Or why dost thou set at naught thy brother? For we shall all stand before the judgment seat of Christ. For it is written, As I live, saith the Lord, every knee shall bow to Me and every tongue shall confess to God. So then everyone of us shall give account of himself to God. Let us not therefore judge one another any more; but judge this rather, that no man put a stumbling block or an occasion to fall in his brother's way" vs. 10-13.

The great tendency is for the strong and the weak to denounce one another and the weaker brother, because of his infirmities, is thus made to stumble. No one is to judge or denounce his brother in those things which are doubtful. Where the Word of God is clear and plain its truth must be declared without fear or favour. It is the great judge, the sole arbiter in every dispute. The circumcising word must be given freedom to circumcise both character and conduct. In things doubtful, however, judgment must be postponed to the judgment seat of Christ. Then all brethren both strong and weak will give account of themselves individually to God.

2.   THE PRINCIPLES BY WHICH WE DISCHARGE OUR FRATERNAL RESPONSIBILITY

These principles are in the highest possible sense Christian principles for they are all related to Christ Himself. The more like Christ we become the more ably we will discharge our fraternal responsibility.

(a) Fidelity to the Lordship of Christ

"For none of us liveth to himself, and no man dieth to himself. For whether we live, we live unto the Lord; and whether we die, we die unto the Lord; whether we live therefore, or die, we are the Lord's. For this end Christ both died, and rose, and revived, that He might be Lord both of the dead and living" vs 7-9.

The common Lordship of Christ over both the strong and the weak must be recognised. In this common Lordship there is the interdependency of every brother. We can neither live nor die to ourselves for whether we live or die we are the Lord's and as the Lord's we are our brethren's. This was the great end of the cross work of Christ, to produce one new man so making peace (Eph. 2:!5). Christ died, rose and revived (lit. "lived again") to be the Head of the Church which is His Body. Every member of that body is not only a member of Christ but   a member of his fellow members in the body and subject to the Lordship of the body's Head. "Every one members one of another" is the scripture (Rom. 12:5)

The proper recognition of this common Lordship of Christ begets obedience in both the strong and weak and a proper fraternal respect in the one for the other.

(b) Fulfilling the Love of Christ

"I know, and am persuaded by the Lord Jesus, that there is nothing unclean of itself; but to him that esteemeth any thing to be unclean, to him it is unclean. But if thy brother be grieved with thy meat, now walkedst thou not charitably. Destroy not him with thy meat, for whom Christ died" vs 14,15.

The word translated "charitably" v. 15 is literally "according to love" the highest form of love, and that love had its greatest manifestation in the death of Christ (Rom. 5:8). We should always view our brethren in the love of Christ and measure our sacrifices for them by the yardstick of the Cross. The destruction mentioned in verse 15 is limited to service and testimony and not of course to the everlasting destruction of the soul from the presence of the Lord.

(c) Faithfulness in the Service of Christ

"Let not then your good be evil spoken of; for the kingdom of God is not meat and drink; but righteousness, and peace, and joy in the Holy Ghost. For he that in these things serveth Christ is acceptable to God, and approved of men. Let us therefore follow after the things which make for peace, and the things wherewith one may edify another. For meat destroy not the work of God. All things indeed are pure; but it is evil for that man who eateth with offence. It is good neither to eat flesh, nor to drink wine, or anything whereby thy brother stumbleth, or is offended, or is made weak. Hast thou faith? have it to thyself before God. Happy is he that condemneth not himself in that thing which he alloweth. And he that doubteth is damned if he eat, because he eateth not of faith; for whatsoever is not of faith is sin" vs. 16-23.

The all important factor in the service of Christ is faith, "Whatsoever is not of faith is sin". Faith begets righteousness, peace, and joy in the Holy Ghost. Meats and drinks can be dispensed with for these are not essentials in the Kingdom of God. Goodbye then, to all forms of sacramentalism and sacerdotalism for they are ruled out completely by this divine principle. To serve Christ acceptably and to be approved of men we must follow peace and the things which build up and not pull down the body of Christ. Godly restraint and abstinence are the hallmark of faithfulness in the service of Christ. The things lawful but not expedient will be refused for our brethren's sake.   Verses 20-22 should be compared with I Corinthians 6:12-13. "All things are lawful unto me, but all things are not expedient; all things are lawful for me, but I will not be brought under the power of any. Meats for the belly, and the belly for meats but God shall destroy both it and them."

(d) Following the Example of Christ (Ch. 15)

"We then that are strong ought to bear the infirmities of the weak, and not to please ourselves. Let everyone of us please his neighbour for his good to edification. For even Christ pleased not Himself; but, as it is written, The reproaches of them that reproached thee fell on Me." vs. 1-3.

We are not to please ourselves but rather our neighbour for his good and our mutual edification. In order to do this we must keep our eyes on Chirst who in His zeal for the Lord's House pleased not Himself but was overwhelmed with reproach. Paul quotes here from Psalm 69:9. The whole verse reads: "For the zeal of Thine house hath eaten Me up; and the reproaches of them that reproached thee are fallen upon Me."

Following Chirst in this, the way of the cross, will lead to terrible misunderstanding by our nearest and dearest friends. The previous Psalm underlines this. "I am become a stranger unto my brethren, and an alien unto my mother's children" (Ps. 69:8).

How much better it is, however, to be a stranger to our brethren and to have the friendship of Chirst than to be friendly with our brethren and to be estranged from Christ. Far better to be an alien in our home and accepted with Christ than to be accepted at home and be an alien to Christ.

"For even hereunto were ye called; because Chirst also suffered for us, leaving us an example, that ye should follow His steps" (I Pet. 2:21)

(e) Furthering the Purpose of Christ

"For whatsoever things were written aforetime were written for our learning, that we through patience and comfort of the scriptures might have hope. Now the God of patience and consolation grant you to be likeminded one toward another according to Jesus Chirst; that ye may with one mind and one mouth glorify God, even the Father of our Lord Jesus Christ. Wherefore receive ye one another, as Christ also received us to the glory of God" vs. 4-7.

(1) Receiving the Promise of God, v.4

Only as we know the promises of God can we further the purpose of Christ.

(2) Receiving the Power of God, vs. 5-6

Only God's power can make us like-minded with our brethren and enable us with them, in glorious unity, to glorify God with one mind and one mouth. This power comes in answer to prayer. Paul prays that this may be granted to the believers by the God of patience and consolation.

(3) Receiving the People of God, v.7

The people of God are a gift from God unto us. As we view them in this light how differently we should receive them. When we meet them in Christ how we ought to embrace them. They are God's sons, Christ's brethren, the Holy Spirit's temples and heaven's heirs. Surely there is no people like the people of God.

[This section finished on Lord's Day, 9th October, 1966, eighty-first day of imprisonment]

15 Our universal *responsibility*

EVERY CHRISTIAN HAS a Universal responsibility to get the gospel out to the whole world. The last command of Christ, "Go ye into all the world, and preach the gospel" (Mark 16:15) has laid a solemn binding responsibility upon us all. A study of the way Paul discharged this universal responsibility in his gospel ministry gives us an example of how we in our day ought to discharge it. Paul, the international soul winner exhorts us thus: "Wherefore I beseech you, be ye followers of me" (1 Corinthians 4:16)

1.   **PAUL'S PREACHING - UNIVERSAL vs 8-13**
      "Now I say that Jesus Christ was a minister of the circumcision for the truth of God, to confirm the promises made unto the fathers: and that the Gentiles might glorify God for His mercy; as it is written, For this cause I will confess to Thee among the Gentiles and sing unto Thy name. And again He saith, Rejoice, ye Gentiles, with His people. And again, Praise the Lord, all ye Gentiles, with His people. And again, Praise the Lord, all ye Gentiles; and laud Him, all ye people. And again, Esaias saith, There shall be a root of Jesse, and He that shall rise to reign over the Gentiles; in Him shall the Gentiles trust. Now the God of hope fill you with all joy

and peace in believing, that ye many abound in hope, through the power of the Holy Ghost."

Paul's preaching was not bounded by national nor by racial boundaries. He was a preacher of Jesus Christ and Christ was the Universal Saviour, "the Saviour of the world" (John 4:42). In these verses Paul dwells upon the twofold purpose of Christ and the conclusion which must be drawn from that great redeeming purpose. Jesus Christ was a minister of the circumcision that the truth of the promises made to the Jewish fathers might be confirmed. He came to deliver His people Israel from a greater slavery than that of Egypt. He was the Prophet like unto Moses (Deut. 18:15) who accomplished a far greater Exodus for Israel. Jesus Christ was not only the deliverer of His own people but the great Emancipator of all the races of the world. The redeemed Gentiles can also glorify God for His mercy.

This very twofold purpose of Christ was the pre-heavenly vision of old father Simeon who said, "Lord, now lettest Thou Thy servant depart in peace, according to Thy word; For mine eyes have seen Thy salvation, which Thou hast prepared before the face of all people; A light to lighten the Gentiles, and the glory of Thy people Israel" (Luke 2:29-32).

Compare this with two other scriptures,

"For there is no difference between the Jew and the Greek; for the same Lord over all is rich unto all that call upon Him" (Rom. 10:12).

"There is neither Jew nor Greek, there is neither bond nor free, there is neither male nor female; for ye are all one in Chirst Jesus" (Gal. 3:28).

Christ was told, as the greater Solomon, to ask of God at the beginning of his reign. He was told what to ask. "Ask of Me, and I shall give Thee the heathen for Thine inheritance, and the uttermost parts of the earth for Thy possession" (Ps. 2:8).

These have been given to Him.

Now the Jewish scriptures are divided into three parts, the law, the prophets and the psalms. See Luke 24:44. Paul quotes from each of these sections of the Old Testament to prove the universal outreach of the gospel to the Gentiles.

The Law: Verse ten is a quotation from Deuteronomy 32:43.

The Prophets: Verse twelve is a quotation from Isaiah 11:10.

The Psalms: Verse nine is a quotation from Psalm 18:49.

Verse eleven is a quotation from Psalm 117:1.

What hope these precious promises bring to the alienated nations of the earth! No wonder Paul prays that we should be actuated by this hope, v. 13. With confidence we can thus discharge our universal responsibility.

2.   PAUL'S PURPOSE - UNIVERSAL vs. 14-21
"And I myself also am persuaded of you, my brethren that ye also are full of goodness, filled with all knowledge, able also to admonish one another. Nevertheless, brethren, I have written the more boldly unto you in some sort, as putting you in mind, because of the grace that is given to me of God That I should be the minister of Jesus Christ to the Gentiles, ministering the gospel of God, that the offering up of the Gentiles might be acceptable, being sanctified by the Holy Ghost. I have therefore whereof I may glory through Jesus Christ in those things which pertain to God. For I will not dare to speak of any of those things which Christ hath not wrought by me, to make the Gentiles obedient, by word and deed. Through mighty signs and wonders, by the power of the Spirit of God; so that from Jerusalem and round about unto Illyricum, I have fully preached the gospel of Christ. Yea, so have I strived to preach the gospel, not where Christ was named, lest I should build upon another man's foundation; But as it is written, To whom He was not spoken of, they shall see; and they that have not heard shall understand."

Paul's was a universal purpose. He strove to preach the gospel not only to his own nation but as "the minister of Jesus Christ unto the Gentiles", to the ends of the earth.

The regions beyond were the object of his evangelistic purpose. Where Christ was named, and the foundation laid in the gospel by others, Paul had no desire to labour. He was a true pioneer. He longed to be the instrument of God for the fulfilment of that prophecy concerning Chirst quoted in verse 21.

"So shall He sprinkle many nations; the kings shall shut their mouths at Him: for that which had not been told them shall they see; and that which they had not heard shall they consider" (Isaiah 52:15).

The extent of Paul's labours is staggering. He laboured from Jerusalem and round about unto Illyricum. Illyricum was the name of a very extensive district lying along the east coast of the Adriatic from Italy on the north to Epirus on the south and contiguous with Moesia and Macedonia on the east.

Over seas, across not only the boundaries of countries but of the continents of Asia and Europe he travelled in days of the most precarious transport. When not at sea he journeyed over the land by foot upon roads infested with divers enemies. Nothing daunted, he diligently pursued his gigantic task "to make the Gentiles obedient through mighty signs and wonders by the power of the Spirit of God". At the end of the day he longed to be able to present as many as possible of them to God. This "offering up of the Gentiles" v 16, he had ever before him. In this he was able to say, "I have therefore whereof I may glory through Jesus Christ", (v.17) To this end, he penned the epistle.

"For God is my witness, whom I serve with my spirit in the gospel of His Son, that without ceasing I make mention of you always in my prayers; making request, if by any means now at length I might have a prosperous journey by the will of God to come unto you. For I long to see you, that I may impart unto you some spiritual gift, to the end ye may be established; That is, that I may be comforted with you by the mutual faith both of you and me. Now I would not have you ignorant, brethren, that oftimes I purposed to come unto you (but was let hitherto) that I might have some fruit among you also, even as among other Gentiles" (Rom. 1:9-13)

The epistle made up in a measure for his hitherto unaccompanied purpose of ministering to them face to face. For he continually yearned to "have some fruit amongst them also, even as amongst other Gentiles" (Rom. 1:13).

3.   PAUL'S PLAN - UNIVERSAL vs. 22-29
"For which cause also I have been much hindered from coming to you. But now having no more place in these parts, and having a great desire these many years to come unto you; whensoever I take my journey into Spain, I will come to you, for I trust to see you in my journey, and to be brought on my way thitherward by you, if first I be somewhat filled with your company. But now I go unto Jerusalem to minister unto the saints. For it hath pleased them of Macedonia and Achaia to make a certain contribution for the poor saints which are at Jerusalem. It hath pleased them verily; and their debtors they are. For if the Gentiles have been made partakers of their spiritual things, their duty is also to minister

unto them in carnal things. When therefore I have performed this, and have sealed to them this fruit, I will come by you into Spain. And I am sure that, when I come unto you. I shall come in the fullness of the blessing of the gospel of Christ."

Paul unfolds in these verses his plan for the future. It is still on an international scale. There is no thought of retirement in Paul's mind. It is ever "labours more abundant" (I Cor. 15:10). The desire of many years he has now an opportunity to fulfill. He feels he has no further place in the parts from which he writes and so he determines to visit Rome. He has no intention of making that the terminus however. It will only be a stopping place on a greater outreach after souls. His real objective is Spain and as he journeys there he is going to stop for a season in Rome and then he hopes, after enjoying the company of the saints in that city, to be helped forward by them in his plan to evangelise the world. He must first, however, return to Jerusalem and bring thither the gifts of them of Macedonia and Achaia. These gifts were for the poor of the church at Jerusalem. What a journey he must make in order to fulfil this service! Right back out of Europe to Asia, and then across the sea to Tyre and then up to Jerusalem. The journey of a lifetime all right, but as nothing to this great evangelist of the world. Many would say, "Why turn back for a service which another could easily accomplish?" Distributing a charity collection seems an unimportant task. Paul had learned that it was a vital service without which his purity could not be perfected. "Pure religion and undefiled before God and the Father is this. To visit the fatherless and widows in their affliction, and to keep himself unspotted from the world" (Jas. 1:27).

So in this section of the chapter Paul tells of his plans and reveals the driving force in his colossal programme, "the fullness of the blessing of the gospel of Jesus Christ".

4.   **PAUL'S PRAYER - UNIVERSAL vs. 30-33**
"Now I beseech you, brethren, for the Lord Jesus Christ's sake, and for the love of the Spirit, that ye strive together with me in your prayers to God for me; that I may be delivered from them that do not believe in Judea; and that my service which I have for Jerusalem may be accepted of the saints; that I may come unto you with joy by the will of God, and may with you be refreshed. Now the God of peace be with you all. Amen."

Paul was a giant on his feet because he was a colossus on his knees. He moved in the atmosphere of prayer. He breathed the breath of prayer. He lived the life of prayer. His prayers were not parochial, confined to a narrow space. The outreach of his prayers embraced the whole world. His prayers were contagious. He ignited others with their sacred fire. In verse 30 he longs for this "togetherness" at the throne of grace. Those who would hinder him in the propagation of the gospel he would bind by the might of the prevailing arms of prayer. Paul cares for his own safety and liberty only, that he might be unhindered in carrying the gospel forward. He longs to be acceptable in his ministry. He prays, himself, and urges others to pray to this end. Then he yearns for the evangelistic crusade and the missionary task and requests more prayer that by the will of God he might fulfil the mission to Rome and there experience refreshment - times of refreshing from the presence of the Lord. He concludes the epistle proper with a benediction which epitomises the whole teaching of the letter. "Now the God of peace be with you all." Amen.

[This section completed on the eighty-second day of imprisonment: Monday 10th October, 1966]

16 The postscripts
of the Epistle

THE POSTSCRIPT CONSISTS of the first twenty verses and ends with "Amen".

The remaining verses are the PPS or further postscript ending with another "Amen".

Final recommendation, vs. 1,2

"I commend unto you Phebe our sister, which is a servant of the church which is in Cenchrea; that ye receive her in the Lord, as becometh saints, and that ye assist her in whatsoever business she hath need of you; for she hath been a succourer of many, and of myself also."

Paul recommends Phebe, a ministering servant or deaconess of the church at Cenchrea, to the church at Rome. A woman heads the list of the many names in this postscript, a reminder that women are well up in the service and honours list of heaven. Paul urges the the church to receive her in the Lord as becometh saints and declares that she has succoured many including himself in her ministry. The great apostle was not ashamed to declare that he had been beholden to this woman in his ministry. The ministry of women should not be despised but the women who minister thus ought to be treated with due honour and respect for their work's sake.

Final Salutations, vs. 3-16

"Greet Priscilla and Aquilla my helpers in Christ Jesus: who have for my life laid down their own necks: unto whom not only I give thanks, but also all the churches of the Gentiles. Likewise greet the church that is in their house. Salute my well beloved Epaenetus, who is the first-fruits of Achaia unto Christ. Greet Mary, who bestowed much labour on us. Salute Andronicus and Junia, my kinsmen, and my fellow prisoners, who are of note among the apostles, who were in Chirst before me. Greet Amplias my beloved in the Lord. Salute Urbane, our helper in Christ, and Stachys my beloved. Salute Apelles approved in Chirst. Salute them which are of Aristobulus' household. Salute Herodion my kinsman. Greet them that be of the household of Narcissus, which are in the Lord. Salute Tryphena and Tryphosa who labour in the Lord. Salute the beloved Persis, which laboured much in the Lord. Salute Rufus chosen in the Lord, and his mother and mine. Salute Asyncritus, Phlegon, Hermas, Patrobas, Hermes, and the brethren which are with them. Salute Philologus and Julia, Nereus and his siter, Olympas, and all the siants which are with them. Salute one another with an holy kiss. The church of Christ salute you."

The designations which Paul uses in these salutations are noteworthy:

Designations linked with "Christ"

"my helpers in Christ" verse 3
"the first-fruits unto Christ" verse 5
"in Christ before me" verse 7
"approved in Christ" verse 10

Designations linked with "Lord"

"my beloved in the Lord" verse 8
"in the Lord" verse 11
"who labour in the Lord" verse 12
"which laboured much in the Lord" verse 12
"chosen in the Lord" verse 13

The expression used of the devotion of Priscilla and Acquila is most striking. "Who have for my life laid down their own necks" verse 4.

Final Exhortation vs 17,18

"Now I beseech you, brethren, mark them which cause divisions and offences contrary to the doctrine which ye have learned; and avoid them. For they that are such serve not our Lord Jesus Christ, but their own belly; and by good works and fair speeches deceive the hearts of the simple."

Paul blows a final trumpet blast of warning. Certain men are to be marked men to the church. They are to be labelled and then scrupulously separated from (lit. turn away from).

Avoid never means associate!

These men to be avoided cause divisions contrary to the doctrines which Paul has set forth in this epistle. Rejectors of the doctrines of the gospel we are to reject. They are not the servants of the Saviour but servants of their own stomachs. To them the stipend is all-important. They are deceivers, the progeny of that old serpent the devil who deceiveth the nations. By their good words (lit. "kind speaking) and fair speeches (lit. "praise) they ensnare the innocent.

Obedience is demanded to this scriptural exhortation, "for he that knoweth to do good and doeth it not IT IS SIN".

Final Commendation, v 19

"For your obedience is come abroad unto all men. I am glad therefore on your behalf; but yet I would have you wise unto that which is good, and simple concerning evil."

The church which honours God, God will honour. The church at Rome was such a church. They were wise to that which is good. Blessed wisdom! They were simple to that which is evil. Blessed simplicity! They were characterised by obedience. Being known to God they become known to man.

Final Consolation v 20

"And the God of peace shall bruise Satan under your feet shortly. The grace of our Lord Jesus Christ be with you. Amen."

Triumph was not only sure but sudden. Shortly God would bruise Satan under their feet. The grace of their Lord Jesus Christ was to be with them. What more could Paul say but "Amen". So let it be indeed!

P.P.S.

The Final Greeting vs 21-24

"Timotheus my fellow worker, and Lucius and Jason and Sosipater my kinsmen, salute you. I Tertius, who wrote this epistle, salute you in the Lord.

Gaius mine host, and of the whole church saluteth you. Erastus the chamberlain of the city saluteth you and Quartus a brother. The grace of our Lord Jesus Christ be with you all. Amen."

Paul's close associates, eight in all, headed by Timothy and Luke here salute the church. Verse 21 should be compared with Acts 16:1, 13:1, 17:5 and 20:4. Verse 23 should be compared with I Corinthians 1:14, 3 John 1:5,6 and Acts 19:22.

The Final Doxology, vs 25-27

"Now to Him that is of power to stablish you according to my gospel, and the preaching of Jesus Christ, according to the revelation of the mystery, which was kept secret since the world began but now is made manifest, and by the scriptures of the prophets according to the commandment of the everlasting God, made known to all nations for the obedience of faith; To God only wise, be glory through Jesus Christ forever, Amen."

Three great facets of the gospel diadem glitter here in all their pristine glory.

Note the word "power" in verse 25 - that is the might of the gospel; the word "mystery" in the same verse - that is the mystery of the gospel; and the word "manifest" in verse 26 - this is the manifestation of the gospel.

After having expounded in the epistle, the MIGHT, MYSTERY and MANIFESTATION of the gospel Paul stands back and thunders forth in grand crescendo this great conclusion,

"TO GOD ONLY WISE, BE GLORY

THROUGH JESUS CHRIST

FOREVER, AMEN"

[This section was completed in the dawn of the eighty-third day of imprisonment: Tuesday 11th October, 1966]